God's Message in Troubled Times

FRANK R. CAMPBELL

God's Message in Troubled Times

Broadman Press
Nashville, Tennessee

Unless otherwise noted, all Scripture references are from the King James Version.

Scripture quotations marked RSV are from the Revised Standard Version of the Bible, copyrighted 1946, 1952, © 1971, 1973 by the National Council of the Churches of Christ in the U.S.A., and used by permission.

Scripture quotations marked TEV are from the *Good News Bible,* the Bible in Today's English Version. Old Testament: Copyright © American Bible Society 1976; New Testament: Copyright © American Bible Society 1966, 1971, 1976. Used by permission.

© Copyright 1981 • Broadman Press
All rights reserved.

4222-39
ISBN: 0-8054-2239-0

Dewey Decimal Classification: 224.2
Subject heading: BIBLE. O.T. JEREMIAH—SERMONS
Library of Congress Catalog Card Number: 80-67462

Printed in the United States of America.

To
JANET
who has helped me to find
God's message in troubled times

Foreword

The writing of this book has been a challenge and a joy. During the preparation of these sermons there were two groups of people in my mind. The first were my fellow pastor/preachers who want to share with their congregations the marvelous truths of Jeremiah. Many of them will preach better sermons than mine. I will be satisfied if mine have helped in any way. The other group is composed of laymen and women who want to know more about Jeremiah, and the way this Old Testament book relates to today's troubled times.

My goal was to make these sermons expositions of the biblical text without being technical. The important technical matters I leave with the scholars. I hope the illustrations I have used and the applications I have drawn from the biblical text will help make clear that Jeremiah is part of God's message in troubled times.

There are many people to whom I am indebted. To my wife, Janet, for her encouragement and cooperation while I was writing and preaching these sermons. To the First Baptist Church of Statesville, North Carolina for encouraging me to share my ministry beyond our own church family. No pastor could have a more free pulpit than they have granted to me. To my secretary, Mrs. Frances Fincannon, for typing and re-typing these sermons and never complaining. Every pastor should be fortunate enough to have such a secretary. To Dr. J. Leo Green, my Old Testament teacher at Southeastern Baptist Theological Seminary, who taught me to love the Old Testament. Like hundreds of preachers across this country, my understanding of Jeremiah has been influenced by his inspired teaching. My debt to him is obvious in these sermons.

These are indeed troubled times through which we live. More than anything we need to hear God's message. It is my prayer that these sermons will help many to find this message.

Contents

1
The Call to Preach

Jeremiah 1:1-19

Some years ago, when I was a college student, I spent one of my summer vacations working for the Norfolk and Western Railway in Roanoke, Virginia. One day as I was walking through the shops, I met a high school classmate who was working there. We talked for a few moments and he asked what I planned to do after I finished college. I replied that I planned to enter the ministry, and I was going on to a theological seminary, and eventually I hoped to become a Baptist pastor. The look on his face was one of puzzlement and his reply to me was, "Why do you want to do that when there are so many other things you could do?" I do not remember a great deal about our conversation that day, except that I remember my reply: "There probably are a lot of other things I could do, but this is what God called me to do." Many things have happened to me through the years, but I still believe that I am doing what God called me to do.

I imagine that there were those who thought similar things about Jeremiah, the great prophet of the Old Testament. It is likely that there were those who wondered why he did not follow in the priestly tradition of his rearing, rather than pursue the dangerous and often misunderstood role of the prophet. The answer was that Jeremiah answered the call of God.

The concept of God calling men to be his spokesmen is important. The call of Jeremiah reveals a great deal about the later ministry of this man. His sense of call is the key to understanding his preaching.

Who was Jeremiah? The answers are many. He was one of the

most colorful figures that walked across the pages of the Old Testament. He was a shy, sensitive, human being caught up in the midst of turbulent events. He was a courageous and confident prophet of God, whose moods varied from great elation to deep rejection. He was a man torn by a sense of his own inabilities and a belief in a divine call upon his life to serve. He was so human that most people easily identify with Jeremiah. He appeared on the scene of history at a time when his fellow countrymen seemed bent on destroying themselves. His message was one of warning and repentance. In many ways, it was a heartbreaking message.

Jeremiah was born in Anathoth, a small village about four miles northeast of Jerusalem. This village had been established by Abiathar who served as a priest during the reign of David. Anathoth was a priestly community with its roots probably going back as far as Eli, who was the priest of the Tabernacle of the Lord in Shiloh where the ark of God was. Jeremiah was deeply rooted in historical knowledge of his nation's past. He likely was from a priestly family and it is obvious that the best of Hebrew tradition and training in the home were part of his heritage.

He knew the Mosaic faith, and he knew the preaching of the prophets who had preceded him. Jeremiah's message was affected by Moses, Amos, Isaiah, and Micah. Jeremiah seems to have been strongly influenced by the prophet Hosea. He spent his early years growing up in a community of scholars, priests, and students of God's Word.

Two other factors bear upon an understanding of the person Jeremiah. One of these factors is rural and the other is urban. The rural influence on Jeremiah's life was the privilege he had of growing up in a small town. His messages are filled with imagery taken from nature and from life in a rural setting. It would be wrong, however, to describe Jeremiah as a backwoods, country boy because of the nearness of his little village to Jerusalem. That city exposed him to all the influences of urban life in that day. The capitol city was just an hour's walk away. Jeremiah must have gone there many times to make the necessary sales and purchases. He must have listened to the traders and travelers, thus learning a great deal about the world beyond the borders of Anathoth.

The opening verses of the Old Testament book of Jeremiah help to locate this prophet in time. These verses state his name, his hometown, and indicate that his ministry extended over a period of four decades. These verses also stress the central emphasis of Jeremiah's prophecy, namely that God speaks. God always has a message for troubled times.

For the ancient Hebrew, the concept of a word meant much more than it does now. For the Hebrew, a word was alive. Their word for this is *debar*. It was believed that once a word was spoken it could not be recalled, because the word was endowed with energy which moved it on toward actualization. There was in the Hebrew mind a close connection between the word and the act. The uttering of a word was an event in itself, because the word was alive. The important matter for Jeremiah was that God's word is alive and comes to men. This word is still alive and the function of those called by God is to proclaim the live word of God. It is not a dull word, but a live word. How could a word from God be anything else?

Jeremiah was a prophet because God had called him. Most Christians are aware that all conversion experiences are not the same. The importance of conversion is that a person discovers the glory of God in Jesus Christ and makes a commitment to that Christ as Lord. For some, it is an extremely emotional experience. For others, it is a calm, reasoned conviction that leads to a personal commitment. Still, there are others who have known the joy of a Christian home and church through the years who grow into it so naturally that when they make their personal decision for Christ, it is difficult for them to remember a time when they were not Christians.

It is the same for those who answer God's call to any type of ministry. God does not call all people in the same way. When Jeremiah's call is compared to some others recorded in the Bible, his call seems very timid and somewhat hesitant. For example, the Bible records that both Isaiah and Ezekiel were called with glorious visions of God and many heavenly attendants. Isaiah was overcome by a sense of national and personal sin; and he cried out before God that he was an unclean man with unclean lips. Ezekiel fell down on his face before the reigning God. Jeremiah seemed to have had no sense of personal guilt as did Isaiah, nor was he struck speechless like Ezekiel. Jeremiah experienced no heavenly visions. He said, "Then the word of the Lord came unto me, saying" (Jer. 1:4). Jeremiah did not react with a deep sense of sin or awe at the glory of God. Jeremiah's call was not a vision of divine majesty, but an experience of great simplicity, directness, and intimacy. It probably was the culmination and ripening of the spiritual influences in his home life and his upbringing in the priestly town of Anathoth.

The awesome part of the call of Jeremiah was the realization that God was choosing him for a task. The words of the Scripture are overwhelming. "Before I formed thee in the belly I knew thee; and before thou camest forth out of the womb I sanctified thee, and I ordained thee a prophet unto the nations" (Jer. 1:5).

The word "know" in Hebrew does not convey the idea of academic or head knowledge but rather dynamic or heart knowledge. It is the kind of knowledge that comes when two people know each other. There are times in life when a person cannot exactly prove intellectually what they know to be true but in the depths of their being, they know it is true. That is the sense in which God and Jeremiah communed with each other. God told Jeremiah that he was formed in his mother's womb and sanctified by God. God wanted Jeremiah to know that he set him apart for service. God set him apart so that he could become a prophet to all the nations.

All true prophets speak to the nations of the world. Preachers no longer enjoy the luxury of speaking just to their own group. Sermons that are heard from contemporary pulpits this day should be both deeply rooted in the biblical truth and also relevant and applicable to the world situation. There is something radically wrong when world revolutions go on and great national events take place and the modern pulpit simply repeats a story about a Bible character or incident out of the past. True prophetic preaching proclaims God's Word and the true prophet brings that word to bear on the contemporary situation. Much modern preaching probably does not qualify for the description, prophetic preaching.

The call of God indicated that he had been preparing Jeremiah all his life for his task. The same God has also been preparing Christians today for their tasks. The events of life bring people to the place where they can make a proper decision for Christ. Family life, academic training, vocational pursuits, hobbies, all these areas blend together to help prepare God's people for the tasks God has for them. There is a basic question. What does God want with your life?

Jeremiah's response was extremely human. It was timid and hesitant. Jeremiah replied that he was too young for the job and besides that, he was not a good speaker. The word Jeremiah used to describe himself does not mean a child, but a young man, probably in his teens or early twenties. Most scholars think Jeremiah was between twenty and twenty-five at the time of his call. Jeremiah was not doubting God, he was doubting himself. He listened to the call of God, saw the enormous task, and when he compared that with his own inexperience, it just seemed like too much. Far from being negative, this was a good trait in the young man from Anathoth because it has always been true that the person who realizes his insufficiency will turn to the sufficiency of God. I can testify, from my own personal life, that I usually mess up when I am convinced that I know how to handle everything with my own wisdom or ability. I recognize that, after giving the best I have, I still need what God can do for me. When I ask for his sufficiency and receive it, I am able to do the big task. Some wise person said "Man's extremity is God's opportunity." This is always correct, especially with respect to prayer. Before Christians can do much real praying, they have to acknowledge their total helplessness and absolute dependence on God. After doing that the stage is set for prayer. Then with persistence and practice, Christians become able to understand the will of God through prayer.

To the doubts of Jeremiah, God gave some words of assurance. God replied, "... I am with thee ..." (Jer. 1:8). It is good to be able to know God is there in the midst of the struggles of life. God promised to help Jeremiah do what he called him to do, and what he could not do alone. When God calls Christians to a job, he gives them the tools to do that job. Jeremiah's life and ministry were marked by two great convictions. The first, God had set him apart for the prophetic ministry; and, secondly, Jeremiah always had an honest sense of his own humanity. Jeremiah's whole life was lived within this tension. All faithful preachers can testify to this dilemma—the call and pull of God and the call and pull of the world. Jeremiah struggled in prayer often with God over problems to which he saw no answer, but he arose to his feet from prayer and went forth to proclaim God's Word.

A young preacher, just out of the seminary, came to see me. He related the great difficulty he was having in his first pastorate because of the number of doubts he had about certain aspects of theology. We talked about some of these matters for awhile. I shared my convictions with him, and then finally I asked him, "What do you believe?" He told what he believed and I said to him, "Go back to your church field, go in your study, and get on your knees. Wrestle with God about all the doubts you have. As you wrestle with him in prayer, God will help you to resolve those doubts. When you go into your pulpit, preach what you believe, not your doubts, and in time God will help you to understand the balance between your belief and your doubts." Years later, that young man told me that he wished he had followed that advice more closely. I think my advice followed the model of Jeremiah. He took his problems to God, but he preached his positive convictions to his people. This is the model for prophetic preaching. The true prophet of God is not one who never has doubts; he is one who works through his doubts in privacy with God through prayer. At the same time he is aware that there is still an abundance of positive affirmations from God that he can preach.

Jeremiah was always certain of God's divine authority. God had said to him, ". . . Whatsoever I command thee thou shalt speak" (Jer. 1:7). Those who have been called by God are always aware that it is God's message, not theirs, which they are to preach. No preacher is equal to the task. Preaching is a frightening business. The honest preacher labors long and hard in his study and yet never feels adequately prepared.

Like many, I have worked hard all week and still come to Friday feeling unprepared. That is frightening! But I never have understood how some preachers can wait until Saturday to begin their preparation for Sunday's preaching. Not all ministers are endowed with the same abilities. Some ministers are not good administrators, others are not good at pastoral calling, and many are not qualified to do in-depth counseling. The one thing every God-called man can do, however, is be prepared when he stands to proclaim God's Word. The preacher must clear away time during the week to prepare to deliver God's Word. It is absolutely impossible to be all things to all men all week, and then on Saturday night put together God's Word that will be delivered on Sunday morning. The study of God's Word takes hours and hours of silent retreat away from everyone and into the presence of God. Even after the sermon has been completed, typed, and polished, it is not real preaching until the man of God steps in the pulpit and begins to preach.

There are times when God's Spirit takes such a message and literally transforms it into the Word of God. This is almost incomprehensible to the modern mind, but is a true reality of the Holy Spirit. God told Jeremiah not to be concerned about where he would preach, or what he would say when preaching, or whether or not he had the ability because he was under orders to preach. God told Jeremiah not to be afraid of all the faces that would be looking at him for God would be with him. The world is filled with all kinds of faces—hard faces, bored faces, indifferent faces, sarcastic faces. It is to these faces that the true prophet goes. Jeremiah 1:9 describes the Lord putting forth his hand and touching the mouth of Jeremiah. This action is often a symbol of purification. Likely here, it means God was bestowing the gift of prophecy. It was God's Word Jeremiah was to deliver.

The ministry of Jeremiah was to be both constructive and destructive. It was destructive in the sense that Jeremiah was to be God's prophet of judgment. Jeremiah was to proclaim a message that everything not of God was eventually to be torn down. It was not a message designed to win popularity. He was also a prophet called to proclaim that there would be a time to build and to plant. Jeremiah was known as the prophet of judgment, but he was also known as the prophet of salvation. He balanced both. He laid the foundation for a new faith and he planted some new ideas about God in the hearts of his people. Jeremiah sought to prepare God's people for the coming crisis in the restoring of their new age. He was not a prophet of condemnation alone.

There is an erroneous conception in the minds of many people regarding preaching. It is usually expressed in statements like, "If the preacher doesn't step on my toes, I haven't been preached at or to." There are some people who want to go to church and receive a good sermonic tongue-lashing so that they can feel clean to go back and to continue their sinful life-style. Make no mistake about it, contemporary prophetic preaching does call attention to sin. It also calls attention to the grace of God and the opportunity to build Christian lives. It is far easier to be negative and condemn than it is to be positive and suggest solutions. Good preachers do both.

A preacher was being interviewed by newspaper reporters. He was quoted as saying, "I know what my people want and I preach what they want to hear." In fairness to that preacher, he was referring to certain doctrinal beliefs, but it didn't sound that way. Jeremiah was not like that. He preached what God wanted, regardless of what his people wanted to hear.

After he called Jeremiah God assured him that he was with him. The assurances came in the form of two illustrations of God's power and readiness to carry out his purpose. The events were ordinary sights which, in the context of this young man's call, were filled with great spiritual significance. First, Jeremiah saw a blooming sprig on an almond tree. This was a beautiful and thrilling sight, for an almond tree in blossom was an indication that spring had come. The almond was the first Palestinian tree to awaken out of its winter sleep. There is in the vision of the almond branch a Hebrew play on words. The word for almond tree is *shaked* from a root word "to be awake." Obviously, it is so named because it is the first tree to bloom in the spring. When Jeremiah identified the almond branch *shaked* God reminded him that he was also awake. (The Hebrew word is *shoked.)* In other words, Jeremiah saw the almond tree as awake, and God was reminding Jeremiah that he was awake to the world situation and he was about to act. God praised Jeremiah for his keen observation regarding the almond branch for it probably was not really blossoming at the time. If it had been in bloom anyone could have recognized its blossoms. Although the branch showed little or no signs of life, the prophet knew that one day it would awake. God compared himself to the branch. The people of Jeremiah's day must have thought God did not care what was happening in the world; but, the man of faith perceived that God was about to act. Time was short and God was awake.

This is a beautiful and tender picture. It may have been that Jeremiah was simply walking about his village meditating upon his call and upon the conditions in his country. The situation in the world was so bad that God's presence seemed to be felt nowhere. The religious history of Jeremiah's people contained the promises of God to do something about the situation. This is what the great prophets had said, yet nothing happened. As Jeremiah gazed at the almond branch that soon would come to bloom, God asked him what he saw. Jeremiah replied a branch *shaked* about to be awake. Then God reminded that he was also *shoked,* awake to what was going on in the world. The same God who causes nature to awake on schedule like the almond branch, also awakens on schedule in the realm of history, watching over his Word to see that it is carried out. Jeremiah would often remember this illustration and it would strengthen him in those times when he needed assurance for his ministry.

The second vision was of a boiling pot. There probably was a pot present in nearly every Hebrew house. It was usually used for washing or cooking. The pot usually set on rocks on three sides with one side open so that fuel could be placed under the pot and set fire. The unusual thing about the pot Jeremiah saw, was that it was not level. Its face was tilted away from the north. It was boiling and the prophet thought that in any moment it would empty out its boiling contents. Again, the word of the Lord came to Jeremiah when he asked, ". . . What seest thou?" (Jer. 1:13). Jeremiah replied that he saw a boiling pot turned away from the north. Then God said to him, ". . . Out of the north an evil shall break forth upon all the inhabitants of the land" (Jer. 1:14). The idea seems to be that of a boiling pot in the north tilted in the opposite direction about to spill its contents southward. Out of the north God was to bring retribution against his people because of their sin, apostasy, and idolatry. Someone in the north was tipping the pot toward God's people in Judah. The other nations were to be God's instruments to punish his people. The foe was not identified, but it is obvious from the experience that God was saying to the prophet that he was still in control of all nations and would use all peoples to accomplish his purposes.

In the light of his call and the two assurances, Jeremiah then perceived God saying to him, "Get on with it." He was told, "Therefore gird up thy loins, and arise, and speak unto them all that I command thee . . ." (Jer. 1:17). Jeremiah was to speak God's Word and not leave anything out! The message might cut across popular beliefs of that day but Jeremiah's commission was to preach it. That still remains the charge for those whom God is calling to preach his Word.

The task ahead of the young prophet was going to be hard. Jeremiah was promised that there would be opposition, but he was also promised God's strength. It is interesting to notice that God did not promise Jeremiah that he would always win over his enemies, but simply that he would be with him.

There is a popular idea in some religious circles today that claims if certain words and certain prayers are said God will bless an individual in every way. There is the idea that God wants everyone to be rich, successful, prosperous, and good looking! I have known some young men who believed that God was going to make them millionaires within five years, so that they would be able to retire. They base all of their philosophy for their business on this assumption. Sadly, I have seen most of them fail. How different their approach was from that of Jeremiah. God did not promise Jeremiah sympathy or success, but suffering and ultimately strength and victory. Jeremiah did suffer and so will those who accept God's call today. God does not promise everyone material success; he promises something better, his presence. God promises his strength and in the long run, his victory.

Jeremiah learned from his call and the events that went with it, that God was alive and active in his world. God still is alive and his Word is still effective. The one called of God today still proclaims the criticism of the wrongs of his age and couples it with a confident hope in the future of God. Not only is God at work, but he also has work for Christians to do. He uses nations, events, and persons to accomplish his tasks.

There must have been some times in Jeremiah's ministry when doubts crept into his life. All God-called persons doubt sometimes. There have been times in my life when I was discouraged and depressed. I have doubted my own ability, wisdom, and strength. But I do not recall a time when I ever doubted God's call. This must have been Jeremiah's experience in a much more profound way. When the events of life crowd in and other persons misunderstand, Christians can find assurance if they will remember their call.

My call to the ministry occurred when I was an eighteen-year-old boy. I was preparing to go away to college, with no idea of what I wanted to do with my life. There was a citywide youth revival in Roanoke, Virginia early in that summer of 1954. I attended most of the services and felt God saying something to my life. I watched as some of my friends committed their lives to full-time vocational Christian service. I resisted and finally the revival closed. I felt I was home safe. A few weeks later at my home church, as a climax to its summer activities, some college students conducted a youth revival. I was working for the local recreation department and managed to arrange my schedule so that I worked most nights and missed the services. The pastor of my home church had asked if one of the members of the revival team could stay in our home. My parents agreed, and after a week of some rather disturbing events, I came home on a Saturday night to ask this young man to pray with me about what God wanted me to do with my life. The next Sunday morning during the invitation I went to my pastor and said, "I don't know what God wants to do with my life but whatever he wants he can have." I had little or no concept of the ministry or the pastorate. My knowledge of theology was almost zero. I had much to learn. Through the years of college and seminary and the almost twenty-five years of being a pastor, the thing that has sustained me is the call I heard when I was an eighteen-year-old boy.

God may be calling you to some task. You may perceive exactly what it is God wants you to do. Then God's words to Jeremiah are applicable to you, "Get on with it." On the other hand, you may be like those of us who are not sure what God wants. What we are sure of is that God is calling us. Simply say to him, "Whatever it is you want me to do, Lord, I will do."

2
From God to Nothing

Jeremiah 2:1-13

It is not difficult to recognize a honeymoon couple. They seem to have eyes only for each other and they don't seem to be able to do enough for each other. They are polite and courteous. The man will usually hold the chair or car door for his bride, and there doesn't seem to be any way that one can displease the other. Honeymoons are truly wonderful times. Many wise people have observed that most marriages would be better if the honeymoon somehow could never end. There are some marriages where this seems to be true. I have known some men who bring their wife a gift after every out-of-town trip. That creates all kinds of problems for those who don't. The truth is that time has a way of making most couples forget the love and romance of their honeymoon. Many marriages come to the point where the "I love you's" are seldom spoken. Some couples can accept that and say rather philosophically, that the honeymoon is over and that is the way it is supposed to be. Is it?

Jeremiah used this same idea to describe the problem between God and his people. He took the figure of marriage (in which he obviously was influenced by the prophet Hosea) to illustrate his message. He recalled those early days at Sinai when the covenant had been made with Israel. Israel thought of herself as a bride following God out of Egypt to a land that they did not know. Jeremiah contrasted the early faithfulness of Israel with her present infidelity. Hosea also had seen Israel as God's bride, his holy, peculiar possession. She was alone with her Lord, his holy property. She followed him in loyalty and in love.

The passage in Jeremiah 2 is a pointed one. God is pictured as speaking through his servant. His words are full of emotion. As God speaks through Jeremiah, he remembers the honeymoon years; he remembers the devotion of their youth and their bride-like love for him. Israel followed God, not for selfishness or for what they could get out of it, but because they loved him. They were holy people, special to God and God himself loved them and cared for them. These people followed him out of Egypt into an unknown new land. Israel was close to God. Anyone who tried to harm her had to contend with Israel's God.

What a promising start. Israel was able to prevail against stronger nations. There was a strong sense of God's concern for his people. The Amalekites, the Canaanites, the Philistines, none could vanquish God's people because God's hand was upon his people to protect them and to punish their enemies. Unfortunately, this love and devotion to God did not last. The honeymoon came abruptly to an end. Israel did not finish what she began.

There are some remarkable parallels in the life of many persons in today's churches. Consider the Christian who has an experience with God. In gratitude he wants to do everything possible to show his appreciation to God. He volunteers for service in all the church organizations, attends services every time the doors are open, and talks a great deal about what he is going to do for God. Unfortunately, most of it is only talk. A few weeks later the same person can scarcely be found around the church. A lot of Christians start well, with great promise, but they fizzle out.

God's love of Israel remained steadfast, but Jeremiah pictured God with a broken heart. God was disappointed in his people. Israel was living in open sin. She became unfaithful to her covenant and gave the affection due God to idols. She, in fact, had ceased to love God and her conduct was shameful. In spite of all of the precious gifts, the faithless wife despised the land she lived in and found excuses to sin. In spite of all that God did for Isarel, she despised him and plunged into sin.

What was the basic sin of God's people? When stripped of all of its shiny paper and beautiful bows, everything that made it look good, at the basic core it was the sin of unfaithfulness to the covenant of God. It was usually seen in two forms, apostasy and idolatry. Israel was guilty of both.

Jeremiah began God's message by contrasting Israel's earlier life of faithfulness with her later falling away. Some Old Testament scholars suggest that the overall form of this passage is that of a covenantal lawsuit. The prophet speaks for the plaintiff and brings the indictment which is the decision of the Heavenly King. God loved Judah like a bride, but she failed him. There are two interesting words for love used in verse 2. One word means the love that springs from the inner self and seeks out the loved one. As it is used in this passage, it speaks of Israel's love as a bride for her husband, God. Whenever the word is used in relation to God it refers to his electing love. The other word is usually translated "devotion" or "kindness." It is also a covenant word and describes Israel's faithfulness to the God of the covenant. This word is used about God. It refers to his loyalty to his people even when they are unworthy. This word can be translated "grace." This term sums up, as well as any word, the character and claims of the covenant. On God's side it is the covenant of grace. God gives. He is not under any obligation, but he gives. He provides for the needs of his people. He redeems them, forgives them, and guides them into the full meaning of life. On the human side, this word means loyal love or devotion. Israel had received the covenant and therefore was under obligation to take what God offered with faith and gratitude, and to serve him well.

What changed God's people? What caused them to stop trusting the all-sufficient source for all their needs, and to begin trusting the nothing gods who could not possibly provide? Was it because God had been unfaithful and failed to keep his word? Certainly not. These people, to whom Jeremiah preached, simply turned away from the true God and followed a wrong god. They became so mixed up that they were satisfied with a spiritual diet of nothing. Many of them did not even realize they were missing God.

People today become involved in efforts to increase their finances, their status, or their prestige and their souls shrivel for lack of spiritual food. This is a difficult illustration to understand. What changed Israel? How could they possibly have turned from the true God to an idol? Israel had seen God's power; they knew what he could do. How could they ever doubt?

Unfortunately, that story is the same in every generation. On more than one occasion I have stood in a hospital waiting room with an anxious husband while he waited for his wife to return from surgery. I have heard him say, "I know I haven't lived my life as I ought to, but if God will just take care of my wife, I promise I will be faithful to God." Others even go so far as to say, "If God will spare my loved one, I will bring a tithe to his church and attend service every week." Often the wife is healed. Then the husband forgets his vows and his covenant with God. All of my preacher colleagues could repeat similar illustrations many times over. Israel knew what God had done, sure, but she nevertheless turned her back on him. In the same way, Christians know what God has done, but they turn their backs on him.

Again Jeremiah conveyed God's word, when he asked his people, "What iniquity have your fathers found in me, that they are gone far from me, and have walked after vanity, and are become vain?" (Jer. 2:5). God wanted to know what had gone wrong. Why had God's people gone away from him and walked after vanity? The word Jeremiah used for vanity could be translated "worthlessness." It was one of Jeremiah's favorite nicknames for the pagan deities of Palestine, and it was a deliberate pun on the word "Baal." It means breath on a cold, frosty morning. It comes out and then it is gone. The word here translated means to become worthless. The idea is that the people not only become like what they worship, but they also actually become empty and unreal. Israel had had the true God, and they gave him up for nothing.

The basic truth was that God had delivered Israel from bondage in Egypt. He led her through the wilderness and provided for her needs. He brought her to the land that was in every sense, a promised land. He gave instruction to her leaders about ways to stay close to him. God wanted them to live within the covenant. God did everything he possibly could for his chosen people, but they did not respond by asking how they could know God better. In fact, their response was just the opposite. Israel became so occupied with the more attractive and the less exacting nature of the religion of her neighbors, that she forgot God. Israel forgot not only the covenant she had made with God, but also the God of the covenant. The religion of the one true God is a moral religion which makes great demands on people. Israel could not meet these demands.

The leaders of God's people contributed to this decline in faith. Even the priests did not say, "Where is the Lord?" (Jer. 2:8). Jeremiah's message was "They that handle the law knew me not" (Jer. 2:8). He said, "The pastors also transgressed against me, and the prophets prophesied by Baal" (Jer. 2:8). And all of them, "Walked after things that do not profit" (Jer. 2:8). The leaders of Israel had betrayed their trust.

The religious leaders had no vital relationship with a personal God, and thus they had nothing to pass on. The warning to the pastor/preacher today is abundantly clear. If God's messengers are to pass anything on to God's people, they must first have the message themselves. They must hold on to God and not to a false idol. They must seek God first above every other desire. They must taste the things of God for themselves, and pass them on to others. They should know the message of God. This applies to all of God's servants. Not all of God's servants are equal in ability or endowed with the same amount of natural talents. Some preachers are better in the pulpit than others. God understands of course, and uses all kinds of preachers. What displeases God is the spectacle of the unprepared minister. God's servant may have many shortcomings, but being unprepared to preach the Word and to lead God's people should not be one of them. The religious leaders of Jeremiah's day drew their message from Baal, from nothing. They went after gods that did not profit and the result was horrible. The result will be the same when God's preachers today draw their message from a source other than the true God.

The sin of Israel was worse than the sin of any other nation. God said to go to the fartherest point east, Chittim (Jer. 2:10) or go to the most western extreme of Kedar (Jer. 2:10) and man would never have seen anything like this. Other nations and people worshiped their false gods and were faithful to them because they did not know the true God. Israel's situation was different. She had known the only true God and had exchanged that God for an idol. It was an unbelievable, stupid decision. Israel exchanged the moral God for a meaningless nothing god. The prophet rhetorically pictured all of creation as shocked and horrified by this act (Jer. 2:12).

If persons think that still doesn't take place, then they are either naive or uninformed. A person needs only to read the newspapers of any large city in the United States to find illustrations of God's people who have turned from following him to following other gods. Sometimes followers of materialism exhibit more loyalty in following their false gods, than do those who follow the one true God.

Jeremiah said the people were guilty of two sins. The first sin was that of forsaking the Lord, who had been like a fresh flowing spring that had satisfied their every thirst completely. The second sin was that for their fresh flowing spring they had built cisterns of their own out of solid rock. In chapter 2, verse 13 Jeremiah uses a most meaningful metaphor. He portrays God as a fountain of living water. The idea is full of suggestions. The primary one being that God is the source of all life. God is sufficient for every need the human being has and he satisfies the deepest longings of every heart. It is as true now as it was in Jeremiah's day that only God can satisfy the heart.

I had heard about stories, such as the young man in my study told me one day, but I never expected to actually hear one with my own ears. However, one day a young, extremely successful businessman sat across from my desk and described all of the people whose lives he touched through his product. I was a little amazed at the extent of his influence. He told me about his success and of his income which hovered close to being six figures. I was impressed. He told me of the possessions he had accumulated in a couple of short years, far more possessions than most people could accumulate in a lifetime. Then he looked at me. His hands were shaking and his voice was quivering as he said, "But I am not satisfied. I turn the lights out in my apartment and none of my 'things' satisfy me. What can I do?" It was my privilege on that occasion to talk to him about the Fountain of Living Water, the one who can always satisfy. It is the same God Jeremiah was talking about, but known even more clearly in the person of Jesus Christ. He brings to us the water of life that quenches our spiritual thirst. Jeremiah, with a broken heart, reminded his people that they had forsaken this God who could satisfy all their needs. Think about some of the people you know. Have some of them forsaken God? Do they spend all they have on a bunch of nothing gods who never can satisfy?

Note again how God's heart was hurt. God said, "I remember thee" (Jer. 2:2), and he asked, "What iniquity have your fathers found in me?" (Jer. 2:5). What had God done to deserve all of this? Israel had not only forsaken the Fountain, but they had built their own cistern.

This is the way it usually is. When men reject God they must find a substitute for him. The universal history of all mankind shows that they are going to worship something. When Israel left the true fountain she began to cut out cisterns. Cisterns have water in them too, which may even taste good for awhile, but they have a way of becoming stale and stagnant. Cisterns have a way of developing fatal leaks and letting people down when water is needed. Jeremiah pictured a beautiful fountain with sparkling life-giving water, open to all who want to come and satisfy their needs. However, instead of enjoying the rich blessings of this spring the people of Israel turned away and dug for themselves cisterns in the dry desert. After a lot of suffering they finally get their cisterns completed and then the rains fell from heaven. Suddenly they realized that these man-made holes were worthless because the water ran rapidly away. The cisterns developed that fatal leak or crack and they did not satisfy. What a tragedy. Here people had access to the fresh, satisfying, living water, and they turned away from it, trying to find satisfaction in some useless search. These people that Jeremiah described must have worked hard to prepare their cisterns. Finally when they had finished and saw them filled to the brim with rain water they sat back to enjoy the fruit of their labors. Then something horrible happened. The hot sun beat down upon it, the cistern cracked, and the waters seeped out. All of their labor was in vain.

This always happens when people try to substitute their own efforts for the gifts of God. Nothing is greater then than the gift of God, and in the hour of need for people to trust anything else leads to disappointment. The great truth today is that God is still the source of life. He is still sufficient for every need. He completely satisfies the thirst of every person who comes to him. The life-giving flow has not been stopped. It is still there in the gift of God's Son, Jesus Christ who will give the satisfying drink to those who turn in faith to him.

The cistern was an idol. People of the twentieth century also have idols. They are called by different terms—sports, entertainment, politics, social prestige, accumulation of possessions—on and on the list goes. Whatever people give their utmost allegiance, the most of their time, and the bulk of their substance, becomes their idol. Idols, like cisterns never satisfy. They always run dry and let you down when you need them the most.

Perhaps the most important question to ask at this juncture of Jeremiah's ministry is: why did these people prefer cisterns to the living water? Why would anyone prefer the water from an old stagnant pond to the water that could be found in a bubbling spring? Perhaps the reason was that in order to get the water from the spring someone had to make an effort. Perhaps the spring was located some distance and someone would have to walk to it, whereas the cistern could be built in one's own backyard. Unfortunately, most people follow the religion that makes the least demands upon them. This is a non-thinking kind of religious faith.

In America today some churches are dominated by an authoritarian type minister. This minister tells the members of his congregation everything they must do. He tells them what they are to wear, where they can go, who can be their friends, and how much money they should give to their church; in effect, he makes decisions for them about every part of their life. I find that difficult to believe, but in talking with others, I have discovered that some people will follow orders blindly if someone else will make decisions for them.

The life of God's people was dependent on staying faithful to the true Fountain. Judah's mistake was in rejecting this fountain for nothing. In her own self-sufficiency she created cistern-like idols that never satisfied. "What iniquity have your fathers found in me, that they are gone far from me, and have walked after vanity, and are become vain?" (Jer. 2:5). In turning from God the people went after vanity or worthlessness and became worthless. Jeremiah's point was not merely that people become like that which they love and worship. The vanity or nothingness of which Jeremiah spoke was not a dead thing; it was alive. It was as lively as Israel was and as powerful as Israel's own thrist. The root of this vanity lies within each person. When an individual's life is not related to God as the Fountain of Living Water, he becomes filled with a great emptiness. He is deceived by all that he values, and everything that he puts his hand to will crumble as he grasps it because he is pursuing nothingness and, in pursuing nothing, he becomes nothing. Israel's sin was that they worshiped nothingness and they became nothing. There is a fountain of living water available for each of us. Will we drink from it or will we settle for . . . nothing?

> There is a fountain filled with blood
> Drawn from Immanuel's veins;
> And sinners, plunged beneath that flood,
> Lose all their guilty stains:
> The dying thief rejoiced to see

That fountain in his day;
And there may I, though vile as he,
Wash all my sins away:
Dear dying Lamb, thy precious blood
Shall never lose its pow'r
Till all the ransomed church of God
Be saved, to sin no more:
E'er since by faith I saw the stream
Thy flowing wounds supply,
Redeeming love has been my theme,
And shall be till I die.
When this poor listping stammering tongue
Lies silent in the grave
Then in a nobler, sweeter song
I'll sing thy power to save.

—William Cowper

3
What Will You Do When It All Comes to an End?

Jeremiah 5:31

I imagine that most pastors feel at times like Jeremiah must have felt. I know I do. There are times when I wonder if there are people anywhere in the world without problems. There are days when the phone rings or counseling appointments pile up to such a degree that I almost want to shout "Where are the righteous people?" This is an experience not unique to the ministry. People in many professions know the same frustrations.

The situation in the world does not look a great deal better either. The world is confronted with the massive problems concerning energy, housing, the use of earth's resources, and the enormous problems between people of various ideological and political persuasions. Those persons who try to live their lives with a commitment to moral values and Christian perspective are sometimes tempted to say, "What's the use?" Jeremiah felt this way often.

The fifth chapter of Jeremiah related one such occasion. The theme of the entire chapter concerns the total sinfulness of the Israelites, which made it impossible for them to receive the Lord's forgiveness. The chapter begins with God speaking to Jeremiah instructing him to go out onto the streets and into all of the public places of Jerusalem and look for a man who executes judgment and seeks the truth. This person should be just in his dealings and have a right relationship toward God in his heart. The idea is similar to the story in Genesis 18 in which God agreed to spare Sodom if ten righteous men could be found in it.

Jeremiah began his search for that one righteous person, through whom the whole nation could be spared. He found no one. Jeremiah discouragingly reported back to God after his first search that he had not been successful. But Jeremiah claimed the reason could have been because his initial search was only among the poor. These were people who could not be expected to know God's law. They probably did not know the right way to worship God nor the prescribed systems of worship, so Jeremiah concluded it would be much better if he would go to the great people for they would know something of the way of the Lord, and the judgment of God. So Jeremiah did. He went to the officials, priests, and prophets, the people of his day who would be expected to know and live by God's requirements. But what he discovered was that these people had also broken the yoke that bound them to God. Jeremiah was crushed with his discovery.

This is a good place to be reminded that spiritual problems are found in every social and economic strata throughout society. It is wrong to conclude that people, because of lack of education or family background, or money, are different in their spiritual relationship to God from those who are blessed with all of those things. The truth is, relationships with God are heart matters not material matters; and there are great people among the rich and the poor who love and serve God. Equally there are those who wish to be relieved of any relationship to God among all classes of people. Jeremiah discovered another lesson that God's people today need to relearn. It was that so far as God is concerned, there are not important and nonimportant people, rich and poor people, cultured and noncultured people; there are just people. The life and ministry of our Lord Jesus Christ gave final verification to this approach of God to the human condition. There is an old saying which states that the ground at the foot of the cross is level; that each person, regardless of his background, comes to God in the same way, by faith in his Son, Jesus Christ.

The search for the righteous person had ended and God spoke to the people through his prophet. His question was, how could he forgive those who swear by false gods and who commit adultery? The answer was that God would punish them. Jeremiah spoke God's word that destroyers would come and ravish and plunder the vineyards of Israel because both the house of Israel and the house of Judah had dealt treacherously with God.

God also spoke to Jeremiah and told him that because the people had denied the power of God, and the word that came through the prophets, that now God would make his word a fire in the mouth of Jeremiah to destroy his people (Jer. 5:14). A casual reading of these verses makes the words sound very hard but an understanding of the situation make them most appropriate. It was not that the people doubted the existence of God. The people to whom Jeremiah preached knew full well that God existed. They simply denied his power. *Today's English Version* translates "The Lord's people have denied him and have said, 'He won't really do anything. We won't have hard times; we won't have war or famine.' They have said that the prophets are nothing but windbags and that they have no message from the Lord. The Lord God Almighty said to me, 'Jeremiah, because these people have said such things, I will make my words like a fire in your mouth. The people will be like wood, and the fire will burn them up" (Jer. 5:12-14,TEV). We would call these kind of people practical atheists. They believed God existed but they didn't believe it mattered.

We have a lot of practical atheism today. In fact, we have it both in and out of the contemporary church. Some of it arises because the people have not been reminded of the power of God. Many preachers could use a little more of the "fire" in their messages. I am not talking about noise which oftentimes has no light to it, but I am talking about a fire within God's messenger to tell people the truth. Jeremiah recognized that his people's complacency was something that smooth speech and soothing metaphors would not solve. Speech that was pleasing to the ears of his people would not bring about what they needed—repentance. They had to be awakened from their lethargy, startled with the seriousness of their situation, and by the prophetic word made aware of their condition. If their hearts were dull and unresponsive as wood, then they would be devoured by the prophetic fire. Today a prophetic fire is needed.

The most exciting message in all the world is the message that God wants to send through his prophets to his people. Week after week, and in pulpit after pulpit across the land, this message is proclaimed. It is not always proclaimed with fire however, and that is the tragedy. There are times when I think that the biggest foe of the contemporary pulpit is not badness but dullness. Most of the men who stand behind the sacred desk do so not for profit, but because they believe God called them to deliver his message. However, often these same men do not pay the price of self-discipline, study, and prayer that it takes for their messages to catch the fire of God.

There is no way a man can busy himself six days a week in doing every task that everyone asks of him and then throw together late Saturday night or early Sunday morning a message which is filled with the power and the fire of God. It is true that there are all kinds of people so there probably needs to be all kinds of preaching. There are many kinds of churches. Sometimes I wonder why everyone doesn't belong to the church where I preach, but I know the fact is that different types of preaching are meaningful in different ways to various kinds of folk. So, I accept the fact that just as there are different kinds of people there needs to be different kinds of preaching. While it varies, all preaching should have the fire of God in it. If a man cannot get excited about preaching God's Word, I doubt that he can be excited about anything.

Jeremiah's message dealt with the fact that the sin of his people was unnatural. They not only were foolish and stupid but they were bringing on themselves the political disasters which were about to befall them. The sheer callousness of the people's sins stood out. Jeremiah said, "O foolish people, and without understanding; which have eyes, and see not; which have ears, and hear not" (Jer. 5:21). What the people of Israel and Judah were missing was a sense of awe and reverence in the presence of God. Again, the problem was not in doubting the existence of God, but in adopting the proper approach to come into his presence.

The sense of awe is missing from a great deal of contemporary religious expression. It is reflected in many ways. For example, if someone walked into the sanctuary of most Baptist churches a few minutes prior to the morning worship service he might well be impressed with a sense of friendliness, talkativeness, or the civic club atmosphere, but it is not likely that one will suddenly be made aware that they are about to worship in the presence of the awesome God, creator of heaven and earth. Occasionally, one does enter a sanctuary, and find the people are hushed, engaged in silent prayer, and preparing for the greatest event a person can know, the experience of worshiping the living God.

This is also seen in the way some people address God. I personally am uncomfortable with the language I hear others using in relationship to God. I am aware that God is near and intimate. He is that kind of God, but he is not a buddy, buddy. Prayer in the same way, is conversation with God, who is the Father, but it should also be conversation that recognizes God as God. It is not conversation between two equals striking a bargain. It is conversation between the Creator and his creature with the creature seeking the will of the Creator. Prayer has always been difficult for me, not the rewards and benefits of it, but the actual doing of it, because it is such an awesome and awe inspiring thing to know that I am communicating with the God of the entire universe. Genuine prayer does not tell God who he is and certainly does not tell God what a person wants him to do, or thinks he should do. Prayer that is genuine recognizes mankinds's helplessness, God's greatness, and the willingness of God's people to follow his leadership. Christians must recapture their sense of awe when they come into the presence of God.

The God Jeremiah spoke to his people about was the God of majesty and might who had ". . . placed the sand for the bound of the sea by perpetual decree, that it cannot pass it: and though the waves thereof toss themselves, yet can they not prevail; though they roar,

yet can they not pass over it?" (Jer. 5:22). This mighty God is the
Creator who had set the sand as the bound for the sea. The sand is a
perpetual barrier which the sea cannot pass. The people of Judah in
Jeremiah's day had no gratitude for God's goodness, as seen in all of
his provisions for them. Jeremiah's complaint was, "Neither say they
in their heart, Let us now fear the Lord our God, that giveth rain, both
the former and the latter, in his season: he reserveth unto us the
appointed weeks of the harvest" (Jer. 5:24). It was probably true that
if backed to the wall and asked, "Where does the rain that enables
your crops to grow come from," the people would answer that it
came from God. But its practical affect on their day by day living was
not thought about. They simply ignored this fact and took all of the
goodness and grace of God and his provisions for granted.

Sometimes contemporary Christians also forget. One needs only
to view the large number of people who claim membership in God's
church who use weekends, especially Sundays, to find recreational
outlets in mountains, at the lakes, and the seashore. There is no
arguing with the fact that every person deserves to get away from his
regular routine and to enjoy some vacation time. The tragedy comes
when Christians are so deeply involved in leisure activities that they
seldom remember that all they have comes from God. Jeremiah's
people had eyes but they did not see, and often Christians today do
not either.

The whole of nature was obedient to God, Jeremiah claimed, but
the people of Israel thought they could ignore God. What better
example of the unnaturalness of the people's sin than the fact that
nature observed the law of God, but people thought they could reject
it. This God set the bounds for the sea and subdued all of the chaos
of creation, and yet foolish and silly people did not fear him. Because
of their stubborn and rebellious hearts the people had turned aside
from God. They were not even grateful for God's good gifts like rain.

But just as the ocean could not prevail against the will of God,
neither can people. It is futile to rebel against God.

One of Jeremiah's most vivid metaphors is found in this chapter. It is an example of the moral and spiritual callousness of his people. Again, the *Today's English Version* translation seems to be to the point, "Evil men live among my people; they lie in wait like men who lay nets to catch birds, but they have set their traps to catch men. Just as a hunter fills his cage with birds, they had filled their houses with loot. That is why they are powerful and rich, why they are fat and well fed. There is no limit to their evil deeds. They do not give orphans their rights or show justice to the oppressed" (Jer. 5:26-28, TEV).

These were God's covenant people! If any people should have been faithful, it should have been them; but sin seemed to abound everywhere. The covenant with God was ignored and their relationships with other people were perverted.

Jeremiah compared the people to "fowlers" who filled their cages with trapped birds. Like some hunters who caught helpless birds, the sin of Jeremiah's people was reflected in their setting traps for the defenseless members of society. They were engaged in cheating the less fortunate. This is a reminder of the terribleness of the sin of social injustice. Jeremiah reminds us that whether the sin is not giving orphans their rights or showing justice to the oppressed as in Jeremiah's time, or whether it is a socially unjust sin in the area of economics in our day, it is wrong. It is wrong to pay poor wages. It is wrong for a business person to fail to provide the proper fringe benefits for employees. It is wrong for people to live in substandard housing. Job discrimination is wrong. Racial discrimination and discrimination on the basis of sex is wrong. It is wrong to grow rich at the expense of others, especially those less fortunate.

Jeremiah pictures an evil man as one who had "waxed fat" (Jer. 5:28). He said of these people "They shine: yea, they overpass the deeds of the wicked: they judge not the cause, the cause of the fatherless, yet they prosper: and the right of the needy do they not judge" (Jer. 5:28). The *Revised Standard Version* describes these people as having "grown fat and sleek." *Today's English Version* says this is "why they are powerful and rich, why they are fat and well fed."

To turn a phrase, they lived off the misery of others. People were not created by God to be exploited by other people. It may well have been that the wrongs described by Jeremiah were technically within the law. It may well be the case that some of those matters which are considered to be socially unjust in the area of housing, discrimination, or wages, may be technically within the law; but Jeremiah's prophetic word rings down through the centuries. There is a higher law, God's law. The fact is, when people become fat and prosperous, they usually become so calloused that even God is ignored. Jeremiah found the people to whom he preached stubborn, rebellious, prosperous, proud, and defiant. Neither the power of God, his grace, nor his law could get to them. They had become hardened and calloused. They had sinned. Jeremiah's warning message was that God would take no more. Sin was going to be punished.

But who would warn the people of the consequences of their sins? The obvious answer would be God's prophets, of course. Note Jeremiah's words recorded in verse 30. "A wonderful and horrible thing is committed in the land," or "an appalling and horrible thing has happened in the land," (RSV) or "a terrible and shocking thing has happened in the land" (TEV). The terrible thing Jeremiah saw was prophets preaching lies. It is not certain whether the reference here was to Baal or to the falseness of the message proclaimed, because it was the word of men rather than the word of God. It seems to me more likely to be the latter. Not only were the prophets not proclaiming God's Word, but the priests were walking hand in hand with them. There was a collaboration of prophet and priest to say whatever the people wanted to hear so that the people would not be disturbed and the ministry could be profitable.

Now comes the worst part of all! The people loved this terrible situation. What Jeremiah meant by a "wonderful and horrible thing" being committed in the land, was that God's Word was not being preached, and the people loved it. They had so rebelled against God that they had distorted and perverted all their values, and they preferred the perverted way of life. Evil stood at the center of the life of the people of Israel and Judah, and the evil expressed in the lives of rebellious people one by one stretched out to reach the whole community. Jeremiah saw only one consequence of such an attitude. If the people did not radically change, if they did not turn back in faith to God, there would be catastrophe. The parallels to contemporary society are so similar that is is frightening.

It was a time of ease and soft living for prophets, priests, false spiritual leaders, and people who love spineless leadership. This picture is not too hard for the contemporary Christian to grasp either. A popular religious person in this country openly brags in interviews and on television that he has become successful because he never speaks of anything negative, controversial, or upsetting to his listeners. His words are always meant to be soothing and comforting, and in return he expects total allegience and commitment from the people who follow him. In the process he becomes very rich. The tragedy is just that. Many people do follow him, and he has become rich because of his message that lacks any of the fire of God's prophetic word.

Jeremiah saw God's people rejecting their covenant relationship. They had chosen not to be God's people and the only result could be that things had to fall apart. There was no help from prophet or priest. Whenever prophecy is compromised for the sake of popularity, when the great themes of God's judgment and righteousness are neglected, the people do become spiritually corrupt. In just such a situation, Jeremiah challenged his people with a startling question, ". . . And what will ye do in the end thereof?" (Jer. 5:31). The people had enjoyed their liberty when there was no trouble. When things were going well no one felt any special need for the protective care of God. The prophets and priests were interested in pleasing men instead of God, but when the tragic hours of distress, war, sickness, pain, and death, and all the other unpleasant aspects of life would come, what would the people of Israel do then?

In the light of the world in which God's people live today, that is again a good question. "But what will they do when it all comes to an end?" (Jer. 5:31, TEV).

There are some who think Jeremiah's reference is an apocalyptic one, having to do with the end of the age. There may be some of that idea present in the passage, but it seems more likely that Jeremiah was referring to the eminent dangers which threatened the life of his people at that moment. From where he stood, Jeremiah could see the apparent judgment about to come upon them. The dangers were even more dangerous, because they came from the folly of people who looked at evil, and loved it.

The end was near, not the end of the world, but the end of Israel's life and life-style.

Today the world may or may not be approaching its end. No one knows. But it may be at the end of my life and my life-style. Jeremiah had concluded that corrupt individuals produced corrupt society, and that corrupt societies breed more corrupt individuals, and the vicious cycle is continued.

Jeremiah's message was a description of and a criticism of a sinful urban society. The basic source of trouble was a loss of their ultimate loyalty to God and the lack of a right relationship with God. When loyalties become misplaced and relationships slip, life inevitably falls apart. Unless something is done about it calamity is sure and certain.

But a corrupt society cannot change itself. The only hope lay in acceptance of the message of Jeremiah. Then the people would change, repent, and accept the grace of God.

Many people like their life and their life-style. The last thing they want is for some preacher to disturb them. The world does not want the boat rocked or the status quo changed. What most people want is more of the good life. To their preachers they say, "Confirm our life-style, and tell us what we want to hear. Tell us how lucky we are to have so many fine things in such a fine life. We don't need God right now."

The true prophet answers with God's message for these troubled times. This time it comes in the form of a question. "But what will they do when it all comes to an end?" (Jer. 5:31,TEV).

4
Talking and Doing
Jeremiah 7:1-28

Americans may be the most security conscious people in all the world. There is nothing wrong with that if people seek security in the right places. God expects every person to be a good steward of those people, places, and things for which they are responsible. Christians are charged by God to take care of their family, to plan wisely for the future, and to endeavor to make the present a meaningful moment. However, the advertising media of today suggests a lot of other things about security.

Security is described as the right insurance program with coverage to take care of the family if anything should happen to the head of the household. Security is described in terms of your own home in "the right neighborhood." Security is seen as the satisfaction of being able to drive the best new automobile. Security is shown as wearing certain clothes because they have distinctive look or fit, and the right label. The most common idea about security is that it occurs when there are a certain number of dollars in the bank. Many economists say that financial security comes when a person has the equivalent of at least one year's salary in a savings account drawing interest. If that's true, most people are not financially secure.

There is something to be said for all of these facets of security. Each of them in their way do bring some measure of pleasure, but in and of themselves they are not, and never have been, enough.

Jeremiah preached to people who were looking for security and thought they had found it. He preached to people who went to church. They used the right words, participated in the right liturgies, and thought that would bring them spiritual security. The seventh chapter of Jeremiah contains the prophet's so-called Temple sermon. A similar account of the same message can be found in Jeremiah 26. There are some scholars who consider this to be the greatest sermon in the Old Testament. It does seem to contain the heart of Jeremiah's message. It is the passage that lies behind the words used by Jesus when he cleansed the Temple (Matt. 21:13). Jeremiah's basic message was that the core of true religion was not loyalty to institutions, but was an experience of faith with a personal God. He seemed to have thought that institutions had value in their proper place. However, when they became a substitute for a personal encounter with the living God, they were no good for either the worshiper or the institution.

It is important that this sermon be set in context. Scholars differ on the exact time frame of the delivery of this sermon. It is clear that there is a shift in chronology. When reading the book of Jeremiah from the beginning, it is obvious that between chapters 6 and 7 there is a jump from the period of Josiah to the early part of Jehoiakim's reign. This is a time frame of almost fourteen years. It was a significant period in the life of God's people. Jeremiah's ministry had begun under Josiah. He had preached about the conditions of the time and warned the people of sin, calling them back to God. A monumental event occurred during the fourteen year time span. It is generally accepted that the event was the discovery in the Temple of a book, identified with the present-day book of Deuteronomy. This book brought about a number of the reforms that took place during the time of Josiah. Jeremiah might have waited to see the outcome of the revival that was encouraged by Josiah. He watched the efforts to purify the religious practices of his people, and yet what he saw was a growth in corruption brought about through a compromise with the Caananite cults, especially Baal.

The people of Judah felt secure because of a misinterpretation of God's promise to the house of David. Judah rested her hope in a

Davidic king and Temple. The Temple contained the ark which symbolized the presence of God. They remembered that less than a century earlier Isaiah had proclaimed that Zion was invincible, and that the king should put his trust in the promise to David (Isa. 7).

That promise had been perverted. Under Jehoiakim, Temple worship was seen as a magical guarantee of God's protection. "Trust ye not in lying words, saying, The temple of the Lord, The temple of the Lord, The temple of the Lord, are these" (Jer. 7:4).

Foreign gods had been set up in the Temple, "For the children of Judah have done evil in my sight, saith the Lord: they have set their abominations in the house which is called by my name, to pollute it" (Jer. 7:30). The practice of child sacrifice was carried out, "And they have built the high places of Tophet, which is in the valley of the son of Hinnom, to burn their sons and their daughters in the fire; which I commanded them not, neither came it into my heart" (Jer. 7:31). The Decalogue was broken systematically, "Will ye steal, murder, and commit adultery, and swear falsely, and burn incense unto Baal and walk after other gods whom ye know not" (Jer. 7:9).

The incredible part of this life-style was that while doing all these sins, the people would come into the Temple and assure themselves that God was pleased with them. "And come and stand before me in this house, which is called by name and say, We are delivered to do all these abominations" (Jer. 7:10). The Temple had become for them "a den of robbers" (Jer. 7:11). What a terrible situation! In chapter 7 Jeremiah spoke to the people. He spoke from the gate of the Temple at a time he deliberately chose, a time of great crisis. Old Testament scholars say that Jeremiah must have known that he took his life in his hand when he went up to deliver his tremendous message. The occasion was likely the Fall Festival. Jeremiah had watched the growth of "Temple superstition" and the people's refusal to follow the true God. He had been in favor of the Josianic reformation at its beginning, but had become critical of it in its latter days. Then he openly broke with it.

The people had gathered in the Temple for a special feast day.

There Jeremiah delivered his burning words. Can you picture the scene? There were great throngs of people making their way into the Temple to give offerings to God. There were well trained choirs chanting their liturgies. An outsider walking in would have said that this was truly a great religious assembly. Yet Jeremiah knew something was tragically wrong. The choir sang in perfect harmony, but that did not sound right to the prophet's ears because it was not in tune with God's word. They were probably saying something like, "The temple of the Lord, the temple of the Lord, the temple of the Lord are these," (Jer. 7:4) referring to the Temple buildings. The implication was that because of the Temple they were all safe from harm. These people believed that the Temple and the city of Jerusalem both belonged to God and before any foreign enemy could capture them, they would have to defeat God.

This unusual interpretation of Israel's destiny came about because of their misunderstanding of the prophecies of Isaiah. Some years before when Jerusalem was under attack by Sennacherib, king of Assyria, Isaiah announced that God would dramatically dispose of his foes. When the crisis was over Isaiah said that Jerusalem would be established as the Lord's throne forever (Isa. 33:20). So the people of Jeremiah's day concluded that the city of which Isaiah's prophecy spoke was Jerusalem and therefore their city could never fall. Jeremiah had to tell them how mistaken they were. He said, "You are trusting in lying words. You are singing the Temple of the Lord, the Temple of the Lord, but the Temple will be protected only so long as you are true to the Lord." Not until the people truly belonged to God could their place be secure. It is with that background that Jeremiah took his life in his hands and denounced the sacred worship within the Temple.

Dr. Leo Green, my Old Testament professor, suggested that Jeremiah's sermon was in the form of a legal brief. The brief contained four parts. The first part was a denunciation of the whole priestly program. Jeremiah 7:1-2 are introductory sentences and the sermon itself begins with verse 3. Jeremiah told his people to stop listening to the lies from both priests and prophets. Their message concerning trusting the presence of the Temple as the basis of Israel's security was one of delusion. Jeremiah's suggested solution was simple. "Amend your ways and your doings, and I will cause you to dwell in this place" (Jer. 7:3). This was a time of crisis. Jeremiah stood where the prophet customarily stood in the gate between the inner and the outer courts. There the people could listen. Jeremiah's message exposed the sin of religious leaders and the sin of the common people alike. It was foolish of the people to say "this is the temple of the Lord, this is the temple of the Lord" (Jer. 7:4) as though the repeating of those words had some magical property to guarantee safety. True religion has never been a matter of words. The faith God's people share today is far more than a creed or some special language. Unfortunately, for a lot of people their Christian experience is sometimes equated with the language they use to describe it.

Several years ago a young man fresh out of seminary supplied in my pulpit one Sunday evening at the request of a mutual friend. A pulpit committee in a neighboring city wanted to hear him preach. We had made all the necessary preparation and the service was a good one. There were a large number of people from the neighboring town. I sat in the congregation that night and shared in both the uncomfortableness of the young preacher and the unnaturalness of the situation. I really felt there ought to be a better way to call a preacher. But, since this is how we do it, I prayed for the young man as he preached, and for the committee as they listened. The passing years have not changed my impressions of that night. It was a good sermon, carefully constructed, well delivered, theologically sound, and challenging in its call for commitment. When the service ended the young man met with the pulpit committee in our church conference room. I felt pretty sure that if they based their decision on the sermon, he was almost certain to be called as their pastor.

A few weeks later I learned to my amazement, that they had decided not to call this young man. They passed him over in favor of another man they described as a "stronger preacher." This stronger preacher stayed in their church less than 18 months. When I asked one of the members of the committee exactly what they meant by one man being stronger than the other, he said that the young man who preached in our pulpit that night just didn't speak very much like a preacher." "Well, what does that mean?" I asked. "You know," my friend said, "he didn't use the language of Zion."

However, he did proclaim the gospel! Christians must escape the idea that certain words are cherished in and of themselves. There is no particular religious merit in the way in which certain words are pronounced. Words are symbols that convey realities. Christians do not worship words. Christians worship the living Word. Christians worship God, and God calls for ethical living. In this time, as in Jeremiah's time, there is no comfort in simply repeating words.

The second part of Jeremiah's legal brief, or his sermon, was a resume of God's expectations and promises. It was a rather pointed declaration of God's demands (Jer. 7:5-7). Jeremiah declared that what the people did was important because it showed what they believed. He reminded them that God desired and required ethical conduct and a radical spiritual reorientation of life. He said that the covenant relationship with God was kept best in his people's daily dealings with one another. God's people had to refrain not only from serving other gods, but they also had to give their undivided devotion and attention to the covenant God whom they followed. God promised to let his people live in the land he gave to their fathers, if they amended their ways and their doings. It is good to be able to speak about faith, it is better to live it.

There are some people who boast about how much soul winning they do. I have always been a little curious about people who talk about soul winning all the time, but never seem to help anyone find a deeper commitment to Christ or become closer to him. Many contemporary Christians can verbalize that their primary obligation is to serve God, but the way in which they live their lives demonstrates that God is not first at all. Do people give most of their time to their job, their family, their avocation, or their recreational pursuits? The thing to which people devote the most of their time can become their false god. Where do people spend the most of their time and their money? This could well be an idol. It must certainly grieve God's heart when he sees his people not only failing to trust him, but also giving what they have to various false gods. Jeremiah said that nothing short of a radical change in their heart and life could bring about safety for God's people.

The third point in Jeremiah's legal brief or Temple sermon was a denunciation of the separation of worship from life. Jeremiah thought it almost incredible that his people could go about breaking the commandments, and still go into the Temple, stand before God, and use proper religious words. Jeremiah talked about the people breaking five of the commandments. They had engaged in theft, murder, adultery, perjury, and idolatry. But they still had the gall to come into God's house and say they were secure, they had it made. Jeremiah said, "You haven't any security at all, for you have made the Lord's house into a hangout for robbers. It is nothing more than a quiet place to which you can go for safety after you have committed your crimes." The fact was God was sick with what the people were doing because wickedness and worship cannot be combined together. The breaking of these five commandments amounted to an almost total breach of the covenant stipulations.

The public religion of Jeremiah's day can accurately be described as hypocrisy. The people's lives were violations of the laws of God, yet they still came into the Temple to satisfy their basic religious superstition. They were coming to the right place, the place of true devotion and worship; but, instead of it making them better, they were using it as a way to cover over their moral failures with an outward appearance of religious zeal. The irony was that they probably began to actually believe that they were pleasing God.

This situation is a contemporary one. Late one Saturday night my front door bell rang. A young teenager asked if he could come in and talk for awhile. This young man is now grown, married, and well established in a professional career, but that night he was a troubled young man. We sat in the living room, away from the rest of my family; and we talked about his family relationships. He was serious about his relationship to God and he was shocked over a recent family crisis. He told me a long story, part of it contained this. "I don't understand my father. He is active in our Sunday School department. He teaches a Sunday School lesson every Sunday. He even prays in public when called upon, but my father is a hypocrite. Sometimes he is so drunk on Saturday night he cannot see straight. On Sunday morning we have to be extra quiet while he tries to get rid of his headache, or his hangover, or whatever he calls it. By the time we get to our Sunday School department, he knows the right words to say and everyone thinks he is good; and I think he is a fake."

My young friend was correct. His father was a fake. Time eventually caught up with his father, and he paid the price in suffering and shame, as does anyone who tries to use the house of God as a coverup for their sinful life-style. It does not matter how beautifully you pray, or how talented you are musically, or how well you worship; if it is not real and genuine, there is no security in it.

The final point of Jeremiah's legal brief or Temple sermon contained a description of the destruction which was near. Jeremiah told his people that, because they were unfaithful, God was going to destroy his house. He promised to destroy it as he did Shiloh in the days of Samuel.

Jeremiah's message contained the frightening prophecy that God would send his people into captivity, "And I will cast you out of my sight" (Jer. 7:15).

Some scholars believe the sermon ends here, but surely there is more. The situation concerned people who thought they could commit any violation and still be acceptable to God, as long as they attended the Temple and brought their offerings. They had made God's house into a den of robbers, a place where they tried to find safety and a coverup from their sin. The Temple and its ritual became a substitute for morality. It was as doomed as the tabernacle at Shiloh.

It is likely that the tabernacle at Shiloh during the time of Eli (1 Sam. 1—4) was the center of worship in that day. Shiloh was located about twenty miles north of Jerusalem and was probably destroyed by the Philistines around 1050 B.C. Eli's sons, like the people in Jeremiah's day, cared nothing for the moral demands of God. On one occasion they took the ark of God into battle against the Philistines because they thought it would guarantee a victory for their side. Instead, the ark was captured by the Philistines. Jeremiah used this well known event to show his people that no place was so sacred to God that it could not be destroyed when the people defied God with their lives. Unless the people repented, Jeremiah said they would feel God's heavy hand of judgment. "I will make this house like Shiloh, and will make this city a curse to all of the nations of the earth" (Jer. 26:6).

Jeremiah's sermon proclaimed clearly that the Temple would be destroyed just as Shiloh had been destroyed by the Philistines. He told his listeners that the Judeans would go into exile, just as Israel had gone. "I will drive you out of my sight as I drove out your relatives, the people of Israel. I, the Lord have spoken" (Jer. 7:15, TEV).

Verses 16-20 contain an interesting message. God commanded Jeremiah to cease praying for his people. As a person of prayer, Jeremiah often interceded for his people. However, because the people were corrupt and their repentance seemingly impossible, their judgment was inevitable. God said further intercession was not necessary. One of the basic functions of the prophet was to intercede with God for the people. Jeremiah was forbidden to intercede for his people because God would no longer hear him.

Then Jeremiah used the illustration of the children running around the streets gathering sticks of wood so that their fathers could prepare and kindle a fire, and their mothers could knead the dough and make cakes, "To the queen of heaven, and to pour out drink offerings unto other gods" (Jer. 7:18). This obviously refers to the practice of the cult of Ishtar or Astarte, the queen of heaven, and the goddess of the planet Venus. She was considered the goddess of love and fertility and was worshiped by the Assyrians and the Babylonians.

God told Jeremiah that the people do those things to try to provoke him to anger. But God asked Jeremiah "Do they provoke me to
anger? saith the Lord: do they not provoke themselves to the confusion of their own faces?" (Jer. 7:19). The people brought about their
own confusion. Jeremiah used the word "therefore," one of the
strong prophetic words, to introduce God's reaction of holy love to
human sin. There is a fury that is poured out upon mankind, beast,
and tree; and that fury burns and is not quenched. When people deliberately reject God and his life-style they hear the "therefore" from
God.

It is likely that the words in Jeremiah 7:1-20 were spoken in the
Temple during the fall festival. The prophet turned sarcastically to
discuss the offerings the people used in their worship. Jeremiah was
not rejecting the sacrificial system completely. He was stressing that
God's first and basic requirment was not conformity, but commitment. He said that some offerings were completely consumed by the
fire on the altar, and some offerings were eaten in part by the wor-
shipers. Jeremiah said, "For all the good it does, you might as well eat
all of it." The offerings were not sanctified because they were brought
by guilty hands. Because they were brought by guilty sinners, they
lost their real signifance. Jeremiah reminded the people that what
God had always wanted was not sacrifice, but wholehearted devotion.

Any sacrificial system or worship system must cease when it takes
the place of the genuine worship of God, and when it is not essential
to the central essence of religion. When worship or sacrifice become
mere substitutes for religious conduct, it becomes nauseating to God.
Jeremiah took his people back to the Exodus experience when God
called for obedience and righteous behavior. Jeremiah reminds us
that this has always been true.

To the people of his day, Jesus said, "And why call ye me, Lord,
Lord, and do not the things which I say?" (Luke 6:46). Formalism,

hypocrisy, superstition, open sin, none of these are acceptable in the sight of God.

"Pile your burnt offerings up as high as you like," Jeremiah said in effect. "Those that are eaten and those that are not, for it doesn't make any difference. These things were not a part of God's covenant with you when he brought you out of the land of Egypt. Go back and remember again what God did when he brought you out of Egypt. What he wanted then, he still wants now."

Jeremiah was saying that when the right spirit comes a sacrificial system is irrevelant. Remember the Exodus, when people refused to listen to God's voice and walked in their own ways. They went backward and not forward. It is always true in the spiritual life that no matter how much one goes to the house of God to worship, unless he hears God's voice he goes backward and not forward. Jeremiah closed his words on a sad note (Jer. 7:27-28). Jeremiah did not mean that there was no value in the sacrifice. He was objecting to the times when it was empty of meaning. When the Temple was God's holy house of worship it was a special place. When it became a hideout for a robber it became a sinful place. Worship and liturgy are means of grace, but when they are used by men to accomplish their own selfish purpose, no ceremony can make people right with God.

The basic issue of the great sermon, of course, is the question of security. Jeremiah's countrymen were frantically searching for security. Yet they refused to hear the prophet who told them they were looking for security in the wrong place. Most people today are still long on being practical about basic needs, especially about security. Sometimes this practicality is short on trusting God. People focus on survival and comfort so much that they are alive in the body but often dead in the spirit. Jesus knew that those who would follow after him would have to know that they were living for something besides food and clothes. Survival is not the purpose of life, and life focused only on surviving finally fails. Remember nothing can be guaranteed in this life, not health, not economic conditions, absolutely nothing.

Reversals can and do happen. One moment everything can be fine, with lots of plans about the future. Then, suddenly, these plans are completely changed. An accident can change the rest of a person's life.

Life lived on a human plain is insecure. It cannot be any other way. Yet Christians can work at the basic meaning of life, so that whatever the fortunes or the misfortunes, they can have something to hang on to. They can find something that gives direction and hope. Jesus reminded the people of his day that God was not pleased by their going into the Temple or saying, "Lord, Lord," but by their doing God's will. He reminded them that God cared for the wild flowers of the field and the birds of the sky, and God's people were certainly more valuable than birds or flowers. Why can't people trust God? Why can't Christians work at letting the presence of God be shown in their lives? Why can't Christians accept the truth that a relationship with God is one of faith and commitment?

Security is not found in acquired things or in reverence for a certain book or religious leader. It is not found in any externals. The only security is the one Jeremiah preached about, living in a right relationship with God and living in a right relationship with one's fellowman. This relationship comes by accepting God's call to repentance and faith and obedience. This is ethical fellowship with the living God.

5
The Wish to Get Away from It All
Jeremiah 9:2-9

Jeremiah is pictured here as a tired, discouraged preacher who for a moment, wants to get away from it all. This is a human picture. It probably happens at some time to every servant of God.

Jeremiah, of course, is not the only preacher to have ever felt that way. At times I have wanted to get away from it all. Most people will admit to feeling the desire to just get away at times.

Sometimes the work load of the pastor/preacher is so heavy that one wonders if there is any human being strong enough for the tasks. I don't say that in order to make you feel sorry for me. If I had it within my power to change the course of my life, I would not change the fact that I am a minister of the Christian gospel. One of my more intelligent acts was the moment I turned my heart, my life, and my will over to God for him to use as he saw fit. There have been so many blessings through the years that they more than make up for the disappointments and frustrations. But everyone should know that the load does become extremely heavy at times.

Preachers are human beings and, even in our sophisticated and educated generation, people sometimes forget that. When someone makes a call or demand on their pastor and he does not respond immediately, or has to postpone performing a certain function, often the members of the congregation have difficulty understanding why he does not respond to their beck and call. What is forgotten is that he may have already experienced fifty or a hundred similar requests in recent weeks, or he may not have enough time, or he may be tired.

I can reflect on nearly twenty-five years in the Christian ministry and recall that there have been tiring, frustrating, and irritating experiences. There have been some that appear humorous in retrospect.

I recall one period when I was in the pulpit, fulfilling the responsibilities of the pastor, for thirty-six straight weeks. For thirty-six weeks I preached twice each Sunday and led a Bible study on Wednesday night. In the spring of the year I was away two consecutive Sundays. I spent both of those Sundays preaching in another church and at a college commencement. When I returned the following Sunday, one of my church members remarked "Well, our visiting pastor is back." He really meant it to be humorous, and I took it that way, but unfortunately, there are some people who do feel that way. That story is humorous because most church folks today know that it is not true. I have long maintained that Sunday is not the hardest day of the week; it never has been for me. The physical and emotional toil of preaching is considerable, but the joy of proclaiming the Word of God more than balances it up. The hard days are the Monday through Saturday's involvement with people in their day-by-day life experiences.

Pressures have a way of building on the pastor as they do any other professional person. Many pastors contribute to their own frustrations by making too many commitments or by performing like a workaholic. Some pastors allow their counseling load to get far too heavy. They spend a disproportionate amount of their time listening to the problems of other people, and they become problem-possessed themselves. There are other ministers who get bogged down in the machinery of organization. They create an atmosphere in which everyone who comes to the church "wants to see the pastor." Some pastors refuse to delegate responsibility to members of their staff or to laypersons in the church. They want to attend every committee meeting and be a part of the decision-making process on every matter. The result is a pastor becoming totally bogged down in the mechanics of the ongoing operation.

Some ministers create a problem with unreal expectations of their pastoral role. They set impossible goals concerning visitation, hospital ministry, and crisis involvement with people. The day when the minister could run up and down the rural road, stopping at every house for "pop calls" is long gone. If the modern minister ably handles his administrative and counseling responsibilities, and then ministers to people in their time of need, he will have more than enough human contact. Sooner or later in the life of every church family there is a need for the pastor because of a death, or marriage, or a vocational crisis. A pastor does not need to run around looking for opportunities to "touch base with his people." If he does his job these opportunities will come.

There is also the pressure of denominational affairs. Some pastors spend a great deal of time attending denominational committee meetings. They help do the things which keep great conventions in motion. But it also can create inward frustrations on the part of the minister who is not able to get everything done.

I have not even mentioned the task of preparing sermons. Preachers do not go into the study on Saturday and preach with any kind of effectiveness on Sunday. Sermon preparation is a constant ongoing process that requires hours of diligent and faithful study. The minister also must take time to be with his own family and to keep his own financial house in order. This is no little task for the minister in the twentieth century.

Many ministers can testify that they find it difficult to stay in town and rest. Unlike many of their laymen who can take time off from their job to work around the yard or to work on their hobby, the visibility of the minister creates the impression that either he should be working, or he is still on call. Many pastors, in order to function, just have to get away from it all. In my own experience, the best laid vacation plans have been upset, and many quiet nights at home with the family have been ruined by a telephone call. There have been occasions when I went home and said to my wife, "I wonder if there are any happy people left in the world," or "I would like to meet someone sometime who had no problems." Sometimes every pastor wants to get away from it all.

With this picture etched in your mind, you can identify with Jeremiah. The truth is that Jeremiah's situation was even more serious and difficult than the contemporary one I have described.

The Old Testament picture is one of a tired, worn-out, discouraged prophet in a low moment. He was going through a difficult and dark moment in his own spiritual life. He had reached the point where he wanted to get away. He wanted to be relieved of his responsibilities, and of all the frustrations that went with them. He had been attempting to minister to people whose lives were empty, and who substituted form for religion. He had prayed, preached, and warned. Yet the people remained unresponsive. He was literally sick of those who had made substitutes for the living God. He had given his all and the people had been unresponsive. Jeremiah wondered, *"Why keep at it? These people are doomed anyway, why should I waste my time preaching to them?"*

This incident gives a vivid glimpse into the suffering heart of Jeremiah. He dealt with morally and spiritually sick people. In his ministering to them his heart broke because of their sins. He had said, on one occasion, that if he could find relief in unending weeping for his people then he would weep. He had said on another occasion, "Oh that my head were waters, and mine eyes a fountain of tears, that I might weep day and night for the slain of the daughter of my people!" (Jer. 9:1). The previous chapter gave a glimpse into the heart of Jeremiah. This chapter looks into the life of a tired, worn-out prophet. Jeremiah was heart sick and sorrow stricken of his grief over his countrymen. They had wondered why God had forsaken them. God had replied, through Jeremiah, with a question about why they had provoked him with their idolatry. The people were gripped by fear, grief, and despair. Their dreams were shattered and some of them were saying that God had let them down. It was Jeremiah's unpleasant task to help the people see that their sin and suffering was the result of their own actions.

Disappointed with his people and saddened by their unfaithfulness, Jeremiah had to face them again with a message. Some of his people were guilty of adultery (Jer. 9:2) and this saddened his heart. Even more, there were sins of the tongue, such as lies, slander, deceitfulness, and crafty cunning that had turned his people from a family of God into a congregation of deceivers. He said of his people, "They bend their tongues like their bow for lies" (Jer. 9:3). He was referring to false reports and faithless slander. He compared their disloyal words to an arrow set treacherously against a neighbor with the intent to kill him. "Their tongue is as an arrow shot out; it speaketh deceit: one speaketh peaceably to his neighbor with his mouth, but in heart he layeth his wait" (Jer. 9:8).

Instead of faithfulness, falsehood had become the law of the land. The people had become so ignorant of the will of God that one evil deed followed another. Neighbors had no confidence in each other, but constantly cheated and took advantage of each other. Each neighbor slandered his neighbor. "Take ye heed every one of his neighbour, and trust ye not in any brother: for every brother will utterly supplant, and every neighbour will walk with slanders. And they will deceive everyone his neighbour, and will not speak the truth: they have taught their tongue to speak lies, and weary themselves to commit iniquity" (Jer. 9:4-5). What a sad situation when brothers were all supplanters like Jacob.

Jeremiah's people had perverted good into evil and ironically did not seem to have any desire to reform their conduct. One evil deed followed another. One false transaction was topped by another. It was a dark picture painted by the prophet Jeremiah. Then the prophet called attention to the basic cause of all this corruption. There was no doubt. The reason the situation was so bad was the lack of true religion. There probably were plenty of people going to the Temple to pray and following the forms of worship, but they did not know the Lord. They had utterly rejected God. The intimate relationship with God had been lost completely. Ethical living among neighbors and families was impossible.

That kind of preaching was not pleasant. The context of it was indeed a horrible picture. Jeremiah knew what a relief it would be if he could just get away from all of this, abandon these corrupt people to their own fate, and go lodge like a temporary traveler might do in the wilderness of Judah. In words that ring with hurt and reality, Jeremiah said, "Oh that I had in the wilderness a lodging place of wayfaring men; that I might leave my people, and go from them! for they be all adulterers, an assembly of treacherous men" (Jer. 9:2).

What a relief that would have been. A few years ago I accompanied three fellow pastors to a meeting in another city. We left the first of the week and came back the latter part of the week. It was an inspiring conference and we all felt uplifted. On the way back, as the miles passed on the interstate, and as we neared home, one of my colleagues said, "I feel the load coming back." We had gotten away and lodged in a temporary place, but we had to come back to reality, to the home base, and the load was heavy.

Jeremiah wanted to escape his unpleasant task. Jeremiah did not doubt the fact that God had called him, but the fact was his congregation was not too pleasant. His situation was not too good and he was tired of preaching to the same stubborn people. Jeremiah was saying, "I need another place." The constant movement of pastors between churches is an indication that the spirit of Jeremiah, who desired to get away from it all, is still in evidence in many pastor's lives. There are some men who do need to get away from their present places of service because the situation for one reason or another has become intolerable. I have a file in my office which contains letters I have received over a number of years from friends who expressed a desire to relocate in another place of service. Some of these requests are extremely legitimate. Some men have needed to move, but some of the requests were for a desire to move for no other reasons than just to move. Unfortunately, there are some ministers that have a reputation of not staying in any particular church for long. Sometimes a preacher will leave a difficult situation only to turn his back on what could potentially be a great experience. It seems that the best time for a minister to leave (if the situation is still in his control) is when he is on top, not the bottom. He should leave when things are going well, and he is succeeding, not when things fail. Sometimes the situation does get out of control and it becomes apparent that there can be no progress during a certain man's ministry. Then it is better for the man to leave and another to come in. It is better to admit defeat than to hopelessly go on when there is nothing else a man can do. What is needed is the ability to know when God wants a person to stay or leave.

Jeremiah's brand of preaching was not designed to increase his popularity. Jeremiah was not the kind of prophet who played to the gallery. He, like his contemporary brethren in the ministry, knew the words that could illicit the amens from his congregation. He refused to use them because they were not the words God wanted him to use. He took his life in his hands a number of times when he stood to proclaim God's Word. He was ridiculed; he was made a laughing stock; he was scorned; he was stoned; he was placed in stocks; he was placed in prison; but he remained faithful.

Jeremiah may have wanted to leave the ministry because he thought of himself as a failure. It is discouraging to labor in any field, especially preaching, and to see no results. Many contemporary ministers are discouraged even to the point of thinking they are failures because of the "growth syndrome." I do want to be very clear. I am all for church growth. I also want to state that growth is not the only valid way of measuring success and failure in a pastor's ministry. There are some men in pastoral situations that are definitely nongrowth situations. There are more people leaving some communities than there are coming into them. There are declining populations. It is inspiring to go to conventions and read in denominational literature about the fantastic growth of certain churches. There is no doubt but that the blessings of God and his Holy Spirit are on the ministers who lead such congregations. At the same time, isn't it also true that there are men who are doing God's will in as equally an effective way, but they labor in hard, difficult, nonglamorous, no-growth situations? It is discouraging to work, labor, grow tired, and still see no results. It takes a great deal of faithfulness to do this.

Jeremiah's wish was a human desire. He wanted to find an inn for traveling men, a wayfarer's lodge in the desert. The wayfarer's lodging place usually was a spot with the barest comfort, yet somewhat in isolation. Jeremiah said, "No matter how uncomfortable or how isolated, I would prefer that to living with these treacherous people." These places were usually sparsely furnished because people, as a rule, spent only a night there. Usually there was an innkeeper whose responsibility was simply to keep the inn. He had no personal responsibility for the guests. He could talk to them, or not. He could listen to their stories about travel, or he did not. Whether he chose to be with the people or not, the next morning the people were gone and he carried no ongoing reponsibility for them.

"What a relief," Jeremiah thought, *"If I could get away from it all. I would just abandon these sinful people to their own fate and go and lodge like a temporary traveler might do in the wilderness of Judea."* To put it in a modern analogy, it would be much like the preacher saying, "I just want to go to another town, get me a motel room, watch television when I want to, eat and sleep when I want to, swim in the pool, and have no responsibility for anyone." "Oh, that I might have in the wilderness a traveler's lodging place" (Jer. 9:2a).

It may be that Jeremiah thought, "I'd just like to be an innkeeper." He may have wanted the human interchange with the other people, but not have the responsibility for looking after them. Jeremiah had been involved in the give-and-take of life and now he expressed a wish to go off and sit in the stands and watch someone else fight the battle.

How could a prophet called by God, who had felt the hand of the Lord upon his life, feel this way? Why? Because the people were just an assembly of treacherous people. They were an assembly of deceivers. They engaged in adultery, dishonesty, and cruelty. They had no genuine devotion to God. They lacked a right relationship with God; and, therefore, they had a wrong relationship with other human beings. Jeremiah wanted to be rid of responsibility for them. He was tired of worrying over unresponsive people and of losing sleep over those who would not respond. It does not seem that Jeremiah desired to become a recluse, for he liked people. His desire was to be alone for awhile, but mostly he simply wanted to be rid of the responsibility for the welfare of others. If he could just run out to the motel, be with people when he desired, and yet not be responsible for them (except maybe if he was the innkeeper for one night) then that would suit him well. He would like to talk, laugh, and listen to some stories but then have no responsibility.

One of the happiest groups of ministers in our convention are those men called interim pastors. They are usually retired men who serve churches during the interim, or transition time, while a church is seeking a fulltime pastor. When I talk with these men, they tell me about the joy of being able to preach and love people without any of the responsibility for the ongoing maintenance of the church. It is a happy time in their life. Sometimes I want to say, "Oh, for an interim pastorate!" Jeremiah was tired of preaching to the same old crowd. He thought it would be nice to go to a place where the faces changed and the people would be responsive.

All of the feelings that I have attempted to describe are natural. There is one important question. The question is, did Jeremiah run away? Did he go to that inn? The answer is no. Jeremiah knew all along that an inn in the desert did not exist. He was aware that he could not escape the reality of his situation nor his responsibility in the situation. He did want to run away and be rid of it all. There probably were more than one occasion when he felt that way. It is likely that because of his kind of preaching, the people probably would have been glad if he had run away. The important message is that he could not, and that he did not. There was too much sin and suffering, too much neglect of the goodness of God. He could not go to an inn. There was no inn for him.

In discouraging moments God's ministers today need to realize that there is no inn for them either. Jeremiah may have felt his ministry was failing, but he also knew that no one else could do any better. Today's ministers need to remember that. If no one else can do it better, why should I not be in this spot? Christians today have allowed the "success psychology" of the world to determine their actions. They have heard about the marvelous success stories and the fantastic accounts of riches of television ministers. Some ministers think that unless that success story is repeated at one church after another they are not successes, even in God's sight.

I think God measures success in ways quite different from the world. Compare the so-called success psychology with the success of the cross. A casual look at the life of Jesus would lead one to conclude that it was not a worldly success story. He ended up on a cross, the most cruel torture of his day. Except for an inner circle of people who knew him and his message, the world would have judged him a total failure. It was through the cross that he demonstrated power over life and death. It was through the cross that he would be able to lift all men up to the Father. The person who walks with God and commits himself to living for him can never be a failure.

Remember those who work for the Lord, especially for a long, long time, do grow weary. They are tempted to quit as Jeremiah was. Yet, in spite of all his frustration and his discouragement, Jeremiah stood fast. He said, "Oh, that I might leave," but he also said, "I cannot." At the moment when he thought he could not take another step, or say another word, God gave him the strength to do just that. As long as God's faithful servants will try their one step and say their one word today, God will still be with them to give them strength.

Jeremiah believed that the commission he had received from God was true. God's word to Jeremiah "was like a fire in his bones" that he had to proclaim. The people were stubborn and the temptation to give up was real, but what else could he do? Could his people be saved in any other way? The obvious answer was that they could not. The situation for many of God's servants today is the same. The discouraged preachers should remember that, with all of the frustrations, theirs is still the only message that can save this world.

It remains true that all have sinned and come short of the glory of God, and it is also true that there is no other name among men whereby men must be saved. It is not easy to proclaim God's message to those who are stubborn and rebellious and will not hear. What God promised is that he would be with his messengers. In his lowest moment, Jeremiah remembered the time when God had called him saying, "Thou therefore gird up thy loins, and arise, and speak unto them, all that I command thee. For, behold, I have made thee this day a defenced city, and an iron pillar, and brasen walls against the whole land. . . . And they shall fight against thee; but they shall not prevail against thee; for I am with thee, saith the Lord, to deliver thee" (Jer. 1:17-19). For those ministers who are asking why they have to carry on at such a killing pace today, it is good to find this example of one of God's most courageous prophets. It is helpful to know that when Jeremiah could have left, he chose to stay and to give all of the remaining days of his life and his ministry to doing the best he could for the people to whom God had sent him.

There is a bit of old homespun philosophy that I used to hear from coaches when I was growing up and playing ball. It went something like "quiters never win and winners never quit." Jeremiah, in the final analysis, was no quitter. All of the people whom God has called, he will equip them and be with them through their task. Remember the life of our Lord, who elected to go to Jerusalem and die, when he could have gone off and lodged in an inn somewhere else. He refused to quit on the people to whom God had sent him. May God grant we never become quitters.

6
These Are the Things That Please God

Jeremiah 9:17-24

The world has many standards for greatness. The prophet, Jeremiah, mentioned three that are still valued in this contemporary generation. The three are human wisdom, human might, and human wealth. They are all a part of today's society, especially the latter.

A book entitled *America's Paychecks* by David Harrop reveals some strange ideas about the way people view wealth. His research showed that the starting wage for a bank teller in America averaged somewhere around $6,000. The average annual income for a loan shark was $175,000. A sales clerk in Bloomingdale's Department Store makes about $6,350 a year. The average shoplifter earns about $53,000 in a year. The most famous former Secretary of State takes in about $500,000 a year from his lecturing, consulting, and writing. A popular female singer earns 2.5 million dollars for 72 singing performances in a casino. Harrop went on to say that "salaries are personal and very much tied up in the American concept about what you are worth." Money, the author concluded, is more important to most people than interesting work. I could not help but think, as I read the review of this book, about the numbers of people who had sat across the desk from me in counseling sessions. Some of them had more money than they would ever need in all of their life, but they were miserable. There are some things in life that money cannot do, or buy, and neither can human wisdom or human might.

Jeremiah spoke a word to those who were depending on false

securities. He warned against reliance upon human wisdom, human might, and human wealth. He issued the warning because those three standards are uncertain and unreliable in times of crises.

Jeremiah spoke at a time when trouble had come to Judah. A sense of doom and despair gripped the entire land. Jeremiah cried out "For death is come up into our windows, and is entered into our palaces, to cut off the children from without, and the young men from the streets" (Jer. 9:21). The exact background of the world situation is not totally clear. It does seem that Egypt, Syria, and Babylon were locked in a mighty combat and the little nation of Judah was caught between them. In 601, Nebuchadnezzar's army had suffered significant losses in battle with the Egyptian armies under Pharaoh Neco. The Babylonian leader started for home to refresh and regroup his troops. Jehoiakim, the ruler of Judah, thought it was a good time to rebel against the Babylonians. "In his days Nebuchadnezzar, king of Babylon, came up, and Jehoiakim became his servant three years: then he turned and rebelled against him" (2 Kings 24:1). Jehoiakim's act was foolish.

Nebuchadnezzar had problems in so many other places that he did not have time for a rebellious little country like Judah. He turned the problem over to his allies and they handled it for him. "And the Lord sent against him bands of the Chaldees and bands of the Syrians, and bands of the Moabites, and bands of the children of Ammon, and sent them against Judah to destroy it, according to the word of the Lord, which he spake by his servants the prophets" (2 Kings 24:2). Poor Judah! For Jeremiah it was a clear sign that the end was near. For Judah there was no future and no hope.

In 598, Nebuchadnezzar marched with his own army against Jerusalem. Jehoiakim died and was succeeded by his eighteen-year-old son, Jehoiachin. The seige of Jerusalem did not last long. The Judeans surrendered and then watched as their Temple was ravaged and everything of value was taken from it. Jehoiachin, his mother, and nearly everyone else of any worth was carried into Babylonian exile. Judah was left without leadership and without a land of value. Jeremiah called for the professional mourners to raise their dirge over the city.

Call for the mourners to come,/for the women who sing funeral songs./.../Tell them to hurry and sing a funeral song for us,/until our eyes fill with tears,/and our eyelids are wet from crying./Listen to the sound of crying in Zion:/We are ruined!/We are completely disgraced!/We must leave our land;/our homes have been torn down./.../Death has come in through our windows/and entered our palaces./.../Dead bodies are scattered everywhere,/like piles of manure on the fields,/like grain cut and left behind by the reapers,/grain that no one gathers (Jer. 9:17-19,21-22, TEV).

Jeremiah had warned his people that this would happen: "This is what the Lord has told me to say" (Jer. 9:22*b*, TEV). Many scholars think that this is the best example of prophetic elegy in the Old Testament.

The prophet Jeremiah had previously described the situation of the people and the conditions of the wasted land in which they lived. He asked the question, "Who could understand and explain what had happened to the people?" He was really asking whether the popular leaders of the people could explain, on the basis of their assumptions, why their land was being ruined and laid waste. People were asking this question everywhere. Prior to this time, the prophets and priests had been giving rather comfortable answers. They had been treating the surface wounds of the people without dealing with deeper, more serious problems. Jeremiah saw the problem existing because the people had forsaken God's law and not listened to his voice. They had followed their own desires and gone after other Baals. The prophet suggested that the people will be sent into captivity among "the heathen" (See Jer. 9:12-16.)

The world of today is an extremely troubled world. Many people, not just preachers, are asking what is going to happen to the world, and what is God about to do? Some have turned this questioning into a lucrative business. They travel about the country advertising their ability to discern signs from the times and from the Scriptures in order to prophetically predict the end of the world or, even more remarkably, to know how God is going to act in the future that lies ahead. The truth is these false prophets cannot predict the future, nor do they know the ways of God.

It does not take an extremely wise person, however, to recognize that something is about to happen. One can look at the tragic conditions of the world and draw this conclusion. This preacher by nature, however, is an optimist. I believe that, while the clouds of despair and darkness do loom overhead, there seems to be shining within them the promise of God's new day. I believe this new day is still ahead for those who will, by faith, embrace God and follow him. The world needs to hear Jeremiah's words, "Who is the wise man, that he may understand this? and who is he to whom the mouth of the Lord hath spoken, that he may declare it, for what the land perisheth and is burned up like a wilderness, that none passeth through?" (Jer. 9:12).

Who is wise? Jeremiah came to answer that question in his own person and in his own message. This matchless prophet came to interpret the meaning of those events to his people. He was an outstanding example of true prophetic preaching. He brought God's Word to bear on the contemporary situation in which he found himself. True prophecy does point to the future, but it also addresses current experiences in the light of God's truth. Prophetic preaching is far more than predicting some event may happen in some distant future. Prophetic preaching is taking an honest, realistic look at what is taking place in today's world and evaluating that in the light of God's revealed truth. In the light of that, true prophetic preaching declares God's Word. It may be, as in the case of Jeremiah, a judgment upon God's people because they have not kept his Word nor walked in his way.

The world desperately needs persons who can properly interpret the meaning of the events of today. This kind of interpretation can come only to the man to whom God has revealed himself. God's people today need to be careful not only to know what God is doing, but also to know what God wants them to do. God's prophetic preachers must be aware of biblical history and God's plan as revealed in God's Word. They must also be knowledgeable of what is going on in the world today.

When I was a college student a well-known minister came to our campus to speak to the ministerial group. Following his address we engaged in some questions and answers. One of the students asked him, "How much time should the pastor/preacher spend with popular news magazines and daily newspaper in planning time for his reading?" I remember that this popular, articulate minister said that he wouldn't take more than five minutes a day with a newspaper and the news magazines were scarcely worth more than the time it took to turn their pages. Through the years I have found his advice to be inaccurate.

Real prophetic preaching occurs when God's man is immersed in the events that are taking place in the world. The true prophet is able to bring a different perspective to the world's events than that of the news interpreter, but he is dependent on the media to inform him about what is going on in the world. Nothing is more pitiful than a pastor preaching pious platitudes, while the world burns up or goes to hell. There are too many important ethical, moral, social, family, and ecological issues to be dealt with in the light of God's Word to not have prophetic preaching.

This sermon of Jeremiah was prophetic preaching at its best. This sermon was a prophetic elegy. In 9:21-22 Jeremiah used the figure of death as a reaper and it has been used as a symbol of death ever since. It may well have originated with the prophet Jeremiah. The symbolism has gripped the imagination of men everywhere. "Thus says the Lord: The dead bodies of men shall fall like dung upon the open field, like sheaves after the reaper, and none shall gather them" (Jer. 9:22, RSV). The prophet calls on the professional mourners to come. They were mourning women employed to sing dirges and stimulate grief in others. But Jeremiah told them that the conventional dirges would not be sufficient. These women were instructed to teach their lament to their daughters, and beyond them to the neighboring women. The prophet painted a desolate and terrible picture.

Jeremiah then spoke of wisdom. He had listened to the boasting of those about him and to it replied, "If you are going to boast, there is something to boast of. Boast of knowing God." The Scripture says, "But let him who glories glory in this, that he understands and knows me, that I am the Lord who practices stedfast love, justice, and righteousness in the earth; for in these things I delight, says the Lord" (Jer. 9:24, RSV).

Many people are tempted to brag about certain areas of their life. There will always be those people who have superior knowledge, and some of them will always be tempted to let it affect their own egos. Knowledge is a valid and useful blessing from God. Yet, it can become a stumbling block and an occasion for pride. Men often put their knowledge on display, rather than considering their stewardship of it and using it under God's direction for the good of others. Knowledge is a gift from God that is meant to be used, not shown off. There are some teachers and preachers who are extremely knowledgeable; but, unfortunately, they are terribly proud of that knowledge. One seldom knows what they are saying although their words may sound beautiful. The bottom line is that no matter how beautiful it sounds, and no matter how sure one is of the superior knowledge of the person speaking, if it does not help anyone, what value is it?

There are other people who receive great satisfaction from flexing their muscles. They like to show that they have might or strength. It is a great temptation to misuse one's strength. In the text it may be a reference to actual physical strength. It more likely refers to the strength that comes about because of one's superior numbers or weapons. I was a part of a denominational meeting when on one occasion a small band of Christians applied for membership in our group. They were rejected. I felt bad about it. The next day I met a man on the streets of our town and he said to me, "I heard you voted on the losing side last night." I replied, "Yes I did. I felt it was an unchristian act to exclude this group of professed believers from our fellowship when they wanted to be a part of it." He replied that it didn't make much difference what the group wanted, because his side had the votes. That's called flexing your muscles. It is done regardless of what is right or wrong. There are times when I go to the giant religious gatherings of God's people and see ethical and theological issues decided on the basis of a majority vote. It is extremely doubtful that any ethical issue can be resolved in such a way.

There was a third group that took great pride in their riches. They looked for opportunities to show off their superior dress, homes, or whatever would make them look good in society. They were no different from the typical American today who goes to any length to impress others with his supposed status. Americans today are in debt for items they did not want or need, but purchased because they wanted to impress their neighbors. They wanted approval.

Today life-styles often are out of step with the Christian perspective. As Christians we need to take a look at the issue of honest stewardship versus a total secular life-style. One of the Christian's challenges of today is to adopt a new life-style pleasing to God, one that has some sacrifice in it. If God's people are ever to make any impact on this increasingly secular world it will have to come through this basic kind of commitment.

The world of Jeremiah's day was a confusing one. If the passage in Jeremiah is dated prior to the coming of Nebuchadnezzar, it is likely that the men of wisdom were congratulating themselves upon the arrangements they had made that kept them free from Babylon. The men of might, who probably were the army leaders, were boasting of their skill and strategy and noting that the world was at peace, thus demonstrating that they had protected the people well. The large group of those who were becoming more wealthy were rejoicing in their riches and making plans to extend their business empire and make even greater gain. Against this false view of life and this sinful attitude of pride, Jeremiah delivered his stinging message. To men who were congratulating themselves on what they had done, Jeremiah replied that men should never boast in wisdom, power, or wealth.

Be careful not to misinterpret Jeremiah. He was not saying that any of these things were bad themselves. In fact wisdom is much to be desired. In a time when educational opportunities are greater than they have ever been, people who are honest about stewardship should want to secure all of the education they possibly can. There is nothing wrong with remaining in school and doing a good job and being adequately prepared educationally to face the world.

It is not wrong to use the influence of might to affect needed changes in the world. It will always be true that the strong will be those who lead and when the strong are adequately and properly motivated, might can prove to be a great blessing.

Everyone knows that wealth can be a blessing. Some of the greatest Christians in our world are those whom God has blessed with an abundance of material things. These Christians have in turn responded by being good stewards of that which God has blessed them. They have given their money to feed the hungry and to clothe the naked trying to fulfill the words of Jesus.

The point is, when properly used, wisdom, might, and wealth can be and are good. However, when they become ends in themselves, they become wrong. They become like idols. They become the twentieth-century Baals before which people bow down and worship. Then they become wrong.

When this situation prevails it is more important to have a knowledge of God than to have all of the wisdom, might, and wealth the world has to offer. Jeremiah was talking about more than mere intellectual knowledge about God, he was talking of a dynamic personal knowledge of God, the kind of knowledge a Christian has when he comes to know God through faith in Jesus Christ. It is not knowledge in the sense of fact, it is knowledge in the sense of personal experience.

People tend to boast in their achievements. The achievements in science and technology of the last decade have been formidable. Jeremiah's message was that persons ought not to glory in this wisdom. The Old Testament carries the deep implication that there is a contrast between the wisdom of the world and the wisdom that comes through understanding and knowing God's will. If Jeremiah was talking about knowing God through the covenant relationship, it could be said that he was stressing that the religion of humanism is good but not adequate; whereas the religion based on a covenant relationship is both good and adequate. There are two ways to look at the human condition. One way glories in the greatness of mankind, the other glories in the greatness of God. They are going in opposite directions. The wisdom that comes from God is that wisdom which God gives to people when they enter into covenant relationship with him.

The words Jeremiah used in his sermon are covenant words. They refer to the dynamic relationship between God and Israel. The covenant words are kindness or loving-kindness, judgment or justice, and righteousness. This covenant, of course, is grounded in God's grace. "Thus saith the Lord; I remember thee, the kindness of thy youth, the love of thine espousals, when thou wentest after me in the wilderness, in a land that was not sown" (Jer. 2:2).

This covenant relationship is expressed in the love that people have for God. This love for God is expressed in the love that God's people have for each other. The maintenance of the covenant is sustained by practicing justice and righteousness. The result of this is peace. When God's people practice justice, love, mercy, and righteousness their lives are fulfilled.

It seems obvious that Jeremiah was influenced by the preaching of Micah. Jeremiah's use of the terms loving-kindness, judgment, and righteousness in the earth sounds much like the preaching of the great eighth century prophet. These things are known to those who stand within and who are faithful to the covenant relationships with God. It was within this covenant that God made himself known and continues to make himself known. For Jeremiah, there is no kindness, justice, or righteousness outside this relationship. Whatever wisdom, might, and riches there are outside this relationship can lead only to destruction. The one firm peg on which to hold, the one occasion for boasting, the one issue in which people may glory is that of knowing God. The only kind of glory that is valid is glory in God. The people who have found God and discovered him real for their lives have something for which to rejoice. When a person finds the reality of God through Jesus Christ he cannot say enough good about this wonderful new friend. People follow a lot of gods. These gods probably fall in the category of wisdom, might, and wealth; but, they are all little gods and will be judged by the living God. This great God is just and yet loving. When people exercise faith in him they discover how to merge righteousness and mercy, and this great God rejoices and takes delight in those who exercise the attributes of his covenant. Love does triumph.

The twentieth century has its peculiar set of values as each generation before it had. Every human being has his own set of priorities. As in Jeremiah's day, many today still place the power of education or technological achievement at the head of the list and glory in that. There are others who believe that might makes right, and to this they give all of their attention and all of their energy. Still an even larger group believes that the accumulation of things and money are the most important pursuits of life. A really wise person, who took the time to analyze, would discover that there is a real fallacy in this kind of reasoning. All of the wisdom, and all of the might, and all of the wealth may come, but it will also go. Then what is left?

Jeremiah concluded that the only authentic basis for glorying was in God. A right relationship with God is what matters most. When Christians put God first in their lives and when they let him fill them with justice, mercy, and righteousness, then these great things abide.

The things of the world will always prove to be inadequate and unreliable. If people glory in these things they do not know the secret of success. God's people must learn to know and lean on the eternal God. God has such a boundless resource of blessings that he will never run out. He has wisdom, might, and riches at his disposal that people know not of and God, working through human hearts, can never be defeated.

A number of years ago a successful young couple was having extreme marital problems. They discussed them on an irregular basis with me. Late one afternoon I received a telephone call from the young lady informing me that she was taking their small children and leaving town. Late that night I received a telephone call from her irate, angry husband. He demanded to know his wife's whereabouts. To understand the story, it must be said that this young couple had almost everything in life they could want. They both had a good education and they were well trained in their particular field.

They carried real clout in the community and were real movers in the civic organizations to which they belonged. They were extremely wealthy. They had been involved in a number of financial ventures which had proved enormously successful. They had everything except respect for each other and love for God. Because they lacked the latter the first soon deteriorated to a state almost beyond repair.

When the irate husband called I agreed to meet him at my church study. We talked for a few moments that night about some of the things that were going wrong in his life and then I suggested that for all of his wisdom, influence, and riches, he lacked a personal relationship with Jesus Christ. I told him that without that relationship I doubted if he had a chance with anything in his life, much less with his marriage. I suggested that we pray. We got down on our knees as we prayed. He arose from his knees a changed man. Soon he was reunited with his wife and they used their considerable talents to help others. They let their influence count in helping the community to be a better place. They became good stewards of the material blessings God had given to them. The last time I saw them they were happy together.

"Let not the wise man glory in his wisdom, neither let the mighty man glory in his might, let not the rich man glory in his riches: But let him that glorieth glory in this, that he understandeth and knoweth me, that I am the Lord which exercise lovingkindness, judgment, and righteousness, in the earth: for in these things I delight, saith the Lord" (Jer. 9:23-24).

7
Lessons Learned from the Potter and the Clay
Jeremiah 18:1-12

A young, dedicated, professional man in our church asked for an appointment to talk with me. He was an extremely consciencious Christian and enthusiastically wanted to impart his expertise and his know-how to others. He had volunteered to help train Sunday School teachers. He had been unable to attract large numbers to the teacher training class, but, in my judgment, he was doing a good piece of work. When he arrived for his appointment, he told me of his discouragement. He was disappointed over the small number of people who had responded to the opportunity to sharpen their Christian teaching skills. He felt that in general there was not a response to his leadership. He felt extremely discouraged. His feeling was by no means uncommon. That feeling has been experienced by God's people throughout the generations. It was the feeling that Jeremiah described in the eighteenth chapter of his prophecy.

Jeremiah was going through another stormy time of doubt and uncertainty. For perhaps twenty-five years he had sought to fulfill the call he had heard from God. He had proclaimed God's Word in the midst of his rapidly changing world. He had used every method he knew. He preached, he condemned, he acted out parables, he plead, and he interceded for his people. Yet, after a quarter century of preaching, Jeremiah looked and it appeared his people were worse off instead of better. Jeremiah began to feel the situation was hopeless and that the captivity of his people was inevitable.

But this idea caused him considerable problems. If, in fact, God had called him, and Jeremiah believed he had; and if it had been God's purpose to redeem his people, what had happened? Had God failed? Was God disappointed with Israel and thus casting her off forever? And if God was forgetting Israel, what happened to his promises? It was a difficult time for God's prophet. It was a time that the strongest and best of God's people go through, a time of torturing uncertainty.

It is sad to see people of great faith lose heart and hope. Yet, in all honesty, it has happened before. The Bible tells this story more than once. It tells the story of the great king, David, fleeing for his life. It tells the story of Elijah, conquering the prophets of Baal, but running to the wilderness to escape the threats of one woman. It describes John the Baptist's moments of second thought and doubt while he was in prison. The Bible even reveals the words of our Lord from the cross when he asked if God had forsaken him.

Jeremiah was down in spirit because the lives of his people were marred by mistakes, failures, weaknesses, and sins. He loved his people so much that their plight caused his heart to almost break. It was in this discouragement that God led him to a certain place to learn a certain lesson. As he watched he learned a lesson which he would never forget, one which would remain with him for the rest of his ministry.

Jeremiah may have been in meditation trying to make sense of what was happening, when he heard the divine call from God within his own mind and heart. "Arise, and go down to the potter's house, and there I will cause thee to hear my words" (Jer. 18:2). The potter's house! Jeremiah knew where that was. How could God give him a message at the potter's house? The Temple, yes; the place of prayer, yes; but the potter's house? The potter's house was probably the workshop or factory in which the potter made his vessels. Probably the place was located in the Hinnom Valley south of Jerusalem.

Jeremiah was familiar with the place God said for him to go, he just didn't understand why he should go. That is why this is such an important passage. The passage reveals a great many things, and one of them is that it describes the way God gives his message to his prophets. It says something about the method of inspiration. Here is an account of the way God caused truth to be born in the heart and mind of one of his prophets, not in the place of prayer or formal worship, but in the everyday occurrance of an everyday workshop. The prophet was able to view a common experience and put it into the profound words of revelation.

This story also reveals a great deal about a problem which Christians still wrestle with, the relationship between the sovereignty of God and the freedom of man. This sermon will not attempt to explain this, but will state simply the conviction of this preacher that both are true. God is the absolute sovereign ruler of this universe. That is a fact. Yet it is also a fact that a person is free to decide his own directions. God is sovereign in his own right but he chooses to work with free people. A person is free in his own right but only free to choose the response that he will make to God.

Jeremiah was at a low ebb and he needed the lessons that the busy professional potter could teach him. He went to the potter's house and watched the man, the clay, and the wheel. The potter was a craftsman carrying out his purpose with the best equipment available. The potter's wheel probably consisted of two stone discs with a heavier one below to give momentum and a lighter one above for shaping the clay. Jeremiah was familiar with the potter's wheel. He was not familiar with the truth he was to draw from it, a picture of God's sovereignty, patience, freedom, and of his determination to carry out his eternal purpose. There was nothing in the clay itself that could make a beautiful vessel. The wheel was of no value except as the hands of the potter guided it. Both clay and wheel were under the control of the potter, as God is the supreme figure of life and his purpose will ultimately be carried out.

The lessons from this marvelous Old Testament story are familiar to students of the Bible. The setting is this: Judah had sinned. She had committed spiritual adultery by going off after other gods. The nation had been through a terrible period of apostasy under Manasseh. But God still held out the gracious invitation for his people to return to him. Judah was like the clay pot that had been ruined, but God could still make of her something good and useful.

Unfortunately the reply of the people indicated the direction Judah would take in the future. "They will answer, 'No, why should we? We will all be just as stubborn and evil as we want to be' " (Jer. 18:12, TEV). The people would not listen to Jeremiah. They would not change their ways. They acted after "the imagination of his evil heart" (Jer. 18:12b). Jeremiah could see what was coming. God was going to send judgment on his people.

Now back to the potter's house, where Jeremiah was to learn more about following the God to whom he had committed his all. Many Old Testament commentators have listed the lessons Jeremiah learned at the potter's house. With acknowledgments to all the list I have read or heard, here are mine.

Jeremiah's first lesson was: the potter had a purpose. He also learned that God has a purpose for every life. The picture formed in Jeremiah's mind was that God was the potter at the wheel of life. Despite what it looked like in the ongoing, day by day world, it was still God's world. It was a time of crisis. It was a time when the people were confused. Changes brought about by conquering nations were coming far too fast, but Jeremiah concluded that God had a purpose for life, and the wise man sought that purpose and related his life to it. Simply stated, just as the potter has a plan for the clay, God has a plan for every life.

The potter used the wheel and God uses the various ways open to him. People never know fully what God is getting them ready for. They simply need to be open and willing to respond. Christians should consider these questions: Have I thoughtfully tried to find God's will? Have I been willing to place my life into his hands, as the clay is held in the hands of the potter? Am I willing to let my life be molded and made over by the grace of God?

A successful man in our city resigned from the board of directors of a well-known company. He did it at considerable financial loss and the risk of being misunderstood in the community. He talked to me and told me about some business practices which he thought were unethical and out of harmony with his attempt to live a Christian life. He had tried to change the system from within, but was prevented from it by the majority of the board of directors. He became convinced that God wanted him to register a protest through his personal sacrifice by means of his resignation. His resignation was a courageous act.

His business suffered. His family knew the stress of changing their personal life-style. The passing of time, however, confirmed the rightness of this man's decision. He was later reemployed by this company and eventually elevated to the chairman of the board of directors. To this day he attributes his success to his belief that God had a plan for his life, and he followed it. Are you?

The second lesson in this biblical story is: the clay can be marred in the hand of the potter. The potter's purpose can be perverted. God's plans and purposes for his people can be marred and perverted.

God has a plan for every person just as he did for Jeremiah, or for all of Israel. When the potter begins his work with a piece of clay he has in his mind a concept of what the finished product will look like. God does the same with a human life. However, the clay can be marred. "And the vessel that he made of clay was marred in the hand of the potter" (Jer. 18:4). Even though God has nothing but good in mind for every life, something else can mar that life. It can happen when people resist the will of God. It can happen when people say no to God's call in their life. God's will can be voided.

In order for God's will to be worked out perfectly, people must cooperate with him. While God is sovereign, he has granted people the freedom to say yes or no. It is a person's response that determines the success or failure of some of God's best plans. Some people find it difficult to comprehend that the great God of the universe granted humans that much freedom of choice. But, God did and that is why choices are important.

Many nations mar the plans of God. They become intent on greatness. They invade other countries and take advantage of weaker nations. The United States needs to recognize that the power and strength it has is a gift from God and must be used properly. While this nation is beset with problems at home, and tempted to turn in on its self and solve the problems to the exclusion of the world; America must be reminded that God's love extends to all his creatures and all the world.

Churches can mar the plan of God. At times people are casual in their discussion of churches. They will say of a certain church, "It's a great church." That statement can have reference to the size of the buildings, or the membership, or the staff, or the financial wealth; none of which really determine whether a church is great or not. Great churches are those that hear the cry of the world and seek to make the mission of the Lord become a reality in their shared life. Bold churches are not selfish. They do not mar God's plan by turning inward on themselves. When times become economically difficult many church financial committees look for ways to save money. Often someone will suggest a reduction in gifts to any missions beyond the local church. That is the wrong place to make a cut. It violates Christ's Great Commission and mars God's bold plan for the world. If it is true, and it is, that individuals can mar God's will for their lives by not being good and faithful stewards of their resources, then the same must be true for churches. God's tithes and offerings, brought by his people, are not meant to be used exclusively to keep the home base secure. They are meant to be used to tell the story of Christ's love. Churches proclaim God's message in troubled times by being honest stewards of their resources. Churches that fail at this point mar the plan of God.

Sometimes families mar God's plans. Families can become self-centered asking only, "What's in it for us." Then they turn in on themselves and become smaller and smaller until they rob themselves of God's blessings.

Individuals can mar God's plan for their lives. Everyone has experienced that. The practice of wrong habits can mar God's will for a person's life and deprive him of the happiness God wants him to have. The misuse of authority and power or thinking more highly of oneself can mar God's will for a person's life.

God's will is not an automatic thing. There are some people who think that everything that happens every minute of every hour of every day happens because it is the will of God. This is not the place to discuss God's permissive will and God's volitional will. Simply stated, God is sovereign and as such he permits everything that occurs, but, what happens is not always his active will.

Early in the pastorate which I now serve, I received a telephone call to go to the home of a family, who were not members of our church. Their small daughter had ridden her bicycle into the middle of the street in front of an oncoming car. The driver, unable to stop, ran over the little girl and killed her. This family was in a state of shock as was the whole community. I went in my capacity as a minister to bring as much comfort as possible in such a difficult situation. On several occasions as the neighbors came in and out of the house, I heard the remark, "This is a terrible tragedy but it must have been God's will. Something good will come out of it. It must have been God's will." I almost wanted to shout. "Why? How could it be God's will for a precious little child's life to be snuffed out without her ever having an opportunity to reach its possibilities? God is not that kind of God. It's not God's will that any of his children should perish. It is not his will that people drive too fast and be unable to stop their cars. This child died because she rode her bicycle in front of an oncoming car. It was an accident, not God's will."

Much of what goes on in this world is not the way God plans it. It's like clay being marred in the potter's hands. To be sure, there are lessons to be learned from it, and some of the experiences enable people to bring their lives into a closer relationship with God. I viewed the death of that little girl, not so much as God's will, but as the marring of God's will due to the mistake of human error and judgment. That's the kind of world in which people live.

The third lesson was: even when the vessel is marred the potter can make another one. The lesson is the glorious truth that the marred life can be shaped again. Jeremiah watched as the potter finished his vessel. He watched him as he examined it. The experience of the potter enabled him to detect a flaw in his vessel that the untrained eye could not see. I have been in the jewelry store and looked at the beautiful diamonds in the display window. When my friend, the jeweler, let me examine some of the diamonds under his gemscope I could see the flaws in them. In the same way, the potter saw the flaws in his creation. What did the potter do then? To Jeremiah's amazement, he took the clay and crushed it. He could have taken it and thrown it on his pile of rejects as fit for nothing else, but instead he took the clay, put it back on the wheel again and shaped it into another vessel. Then something began to dawn on Jeremiah. "So he made it again another vessel, as seemed good to the potter to make it" (Jer. 18:4b).

Jeremiah realized that people can resist the will of God, but it is not God that ultimately destroys them. God takes the stubborn, imperfect vessel and continues to work with it. In fact, he makes of it a new vessel, a useful vessel. Years later, Paul would say "Therefore if any man be in Christ, he is a new creature" (2 Cor. 5:17). Only one thing keeps a person from being useful to God and that is the sinfulness and stubbornness of his own heart. Whenever a person yields himself to God, the great Potter reshapes his life. When God reshapes a life it is never the same.

Jeremiah learned that when the vessel in the potter's shop turned out poorly shaped or spoiled, the potter remolded it into another form. God does that with his people. However, if the clay remained rebellious and would not respond to the design of the maker it had to be broken up and reformed. Here was the great lesson Jeremiah learned. Israel looked like a total reject, yet God was not casting Israel off. He was giving her another chance. Her life as she now knew it was doomed, captivity was certain. However, captivity was not to be ultimate doom, but discipline.

The Bible is filled with stories of men who became discouraged and lost heart and hope. The same Bible is also filled with stories of those whom God gave another chance, people who responded to the invitation for their lives to be remolded. Read the list—David, Samson, John Mark, Simon Peter, and on and on. Their lives slipped and fell but "where sin abounded, grace did much more abound" (Rom. 5:20).

Thus, at the potter's house, Jeremiah learned some valuable lessons that Christians today need to learn. He learned about God's patience and love. He learned that God, because he is sovereign, in his grace will give his people another chance to fulfill his purposes for them. He also learned that God's will ultimately prevails. This was another turning point in Jeremiah's ministry. He was convinced that his nation was doomed, but he learned that it was not absolutely the end. Israel was to be disciplined. Through the discipline of exile and captivity God, like the potter, would fashion another vessel which he would use to carry out his work and his ministry in the world.

God is like the potter. He can adjust to the change in situations and if his people cooperate with him he can make them the kind of people he wants them to be, a real covenant community. However, if God's people refuse to cooperate he will deal with them drastically. He will discipline them in love, if necessary, in order that they might be made over into people he can use effectively for his purposes.

We have all misused the good gift of God's life. Would you acknowledge this day that you have marred your life and that you wish now to hand it over to God to let him remold it and remake it?

8
How Do You Recognize a False Prophet?

Jeremiah 23:23-32

Life for many people seems to be completely out of control. Many ideas that at one time was firm and solid have become soft and slippery. Beliefs that were thought to be pegged down to last for generations have come loose and new ideas fly everywhere. Long cherished concepts are being stretched, torn, and pulled every day. There are conflicting voices, and confusing books. The problems of energy, inflation, hunger, polution, crime, nuclear holocaust, moral conflict, and ethical confusion, seems to go on and on. When times are so uncertain it is natural to look for someone who can give a sure and steady word. Christians look for someone who can give them God's message for these troubled times. As with those before, this generation, logically looks toward God, toward God's servants, his ministers, to provide this message. Christians look and listen but, unfortunately, there is more confusion.

There are many preachers today and yet their messages are different. In fact their messages are quite different. How can a Christian tell which is the true minister of God? How can a Christian tell which man has God's message? How can a Christian identify false prophets? Admittedly, it is not always easy to tell a false prophet from a true prophet. Many false prophets are quite sincere in their opinions and they speak with the assurance that the Lord has given them their message. Jeremiah said the false prophets "speak a vision of their own heart, and not out of the mouth of the Lord" (Jer. 23:16). Jeremiah claimed that God said, "I have not sent these prophets, yet they ran: I have not spoken to them, yet they prophesied" (Jer. 23:21).

Today's generation is not the first to be plagued by the presence of ministers who could be described by the term "false prophets." Some of them have deluded themselves, and many of them have confused others with their lies. Every true minister ought to check his own heart and his own life to be sure that he has heard God's clear call. I would suggest that every devoted lay person in the church be certain that the message from their pulpit is genuinely God's message.

Jeremiah had some good advice about this confusing dilemma. He warned against prophets whose words were appealing and whose advice was easy.

In determining the difference between a true and a false prophet, there is a basic starting question: How does God reveal his word? Jeremiah's answer began with his concept of God. He depicted God as saying, "I am a God who is everywhere and not in one place only" (Jer. 23:23, TEV). Jeremiah started with the concept of the onmipresence of God.

God is not limited in any way as people are, especially in his vision. God can see both what is near at hand, and what is far off. Sometimes when I am counseling, a person's problem becomes so confusing that I have to confess that I do not know the answer. I have told people, "I wish I could go over to the shelf, pull off a book and give it to you, and it would give you all of the answers to the problems that you face. Unfortunately, there just is not such a book." Sometimes I have to say, "Frankly, I don't see an answer to your problem, but I am sure that God does. For right now the only solution I can see is that you should seek the mind and will of God."

Jeremiah also said God knows everything. There is no problem with that. God's presence fills heaven and earth. He is all wise and desires to communicate his will. One of the greatest revelations that ever came to me as a young preacher was this knowledge that God really does know everything. The great God who created all the universe, who hung every star in its proper place, who sends rain and sun, light and day, this great God knows my name. For me that was a

startling and amazing conclusion. Jeremiah knew it a long time ago
and so has every true preacher of his Word since.

Look at the scene for an understanding of Jeremiah's dilemma.
With the coming of the Babylonians, Jeremiah's city was full of
prophets who were making all kinds of favorable predictions calcu-
lated to do one thing, please the people. They claimed to speak with
divine authority, but actually their words were filled with lies and
deceit. Jeremiah viewed the situation and concluded that there was a
great difference between ministry, as he performed it, and that performed by the official prophets. He stated clearly "Their might is not
right" (Jer. 23:10, RSV). Jeremiah described himself as a drunken
man whose bones were shaking within him. Jeremiah staggered like
a drunken man because he saw clearly the sham on which the official
religion of his time was based. He was actually staggered at the falseness of the religious core of his community. Their might was not right
in three ways. It was adulterous (Jer. 23:10); it was doomed to fall
(Jer. 23:12); and these false prophets spoke for themselves, not for
God (Jer. 23:21).

Jeremiah was deeply concerned because it was not just the general run of people who were confused and confusing, but it was the
prophets of God. Jeremiah hurled his challenge to them. Their might
was not right. The land had become full of adulterers. He thought it
was terrible enough that the prophets of Samaria should have been
so wrong. They prophesied by Baal and that was bad enough, but the
prophetic spirit and the true preachers of God in Jerusalem had
deteriorated even worse. They had filled the people with vain hopes
and pious words. Therefore their guilt was much greater. They really
committed adultery and walked in lies. They told the people that the
divine hand of God was on them to protect them, but Jeremiah knew
that judgment was near. They did not try to motivate the people to a
deeper fellowship with God and a better relationship with their fellowman. Instead, they, "strengthen also the hands of the evildoers,
that none doth return from his wickedness: they are all of them unto
me as Sodom, and the inhabitants thereof as Gomorrah" (Jer. 23:14).

The false prophets had committed adultery and they walked in lies. Their moral life was an insult to God. How could a prophet's life be immoral and he still claim to present God's Word?

The life of the preacher is extremely important to his people and to his message. There are some ministers and their families who have been forced to live up to their congregation's unrealistic expectations. Everyone has heard the stories and jokes about living in the fishbowl or the glass house. The situation has greatly improved in recent years, but there is still a sense in which the minister is looked upon by the community as a person who is just a little bit different. As one preacher, let me say to all preachers and to the lay people in the churches that each minister, just like each lay person, has to work out what it means for him or her to be a Christian. This means that the desires of a vocal group in the congregation should not determine the life-style of the minister. Early in my ministry I decided that I would attempt to do two things with my life-style. First, I would try to bring it under the total control of God. To do that I would try to have what I thought was an honest relationship with God regarding matters that I did or did not do. I concluded that I would not let other people tell me what I could and could not do. Once I settled this matter with God, then I was willing to handle whatever criticisms of that particular life-style might come. Second, I made the decision that in my life-style I would not consciously do anything that would cause a weaker Christian to stumble or fall. It has not always been easy to balance these two things, but I have tried. I feel free in Christ. I do not use that freedom foolishly. There are some things that I refrain from doing not as much out of a sense of their being wrong, as out of a desire not to confuse or hinder another.

Many of the prophets in Jerusalem were false and thus the prophetic spirit had been poisoned and "ungodliness has gone forth into all the land" (Jer. 23:15, RSV). The country had become like a Sodom and Gomorrah. It was morally, spiritually, ethically, and religiously corrupt and bankrupt. Retribution was inevitable. Jeremiah used the two vivid metaphors of wormwood, which was something extremely bitter, and the water of gall, a poisoned water, something extremely deadly. Through Jeremiah God said to the people of Jerusalem, "Do not listen to what the prophets say; they are filling you with false hopes. They tell you what they have imagined and not what I have said. To the people who refuse to listen to what I have said, they keep saying that all will go well with them. And they tell everyone who is stubborn that disaster will never touch him" (Jer. 23:16-17, TEV). Jeremiah was saying, "Don't listen to these people. They do not know the Lord's secret thoughts. They have not heard or understood his message. They have not even listened or paid any attention to what he has said. God is now angry with them." Jeremiah claimed that God said he didn't send them, but even so, they went. If they had been of God they could have proclaimed his message and they could have made people give up their evil lives and leave their wicked ways.

Because these false prophets had no moral character they could not exert any moral leadership. The result was that they did not have a genuine message from God. Their message had no moral content or challenge to it. It was the word of man and not the Word of God. They preached peace and prosperity rather than judgment. They proclaimed that all was well when the condition was precarious. They gave their people empty hopes and tailored their sermons to fit their desires and the desires of their listeners.

The false prophets ran about saying, "I have dreamed," thus revealing the self-satisfaction they took in their vocation. Their vocation was the center around which their life turned. They defied their own position rather than seeking to serve God. Their dreams became, some scholars say, a God substitute even as the images of Baal were substitutes for the God worshiped by their fathers. Their progressive deterioration is revealed in God's clear words.

I am against those prophets who take each other's words and proclaim them as my message. I am also against those prophets who speak their own words and claim they came from me. Listen to what I, the Lord, say! I am against the prophets who tell their dreams that are full of lies. They tell these dreams and lead my people astray with their lies and their boasting. I did not send them or order them to go, and they are of no help at all to the people. I, the Lord, have spoken (Jer. 23:30-32, TEV).

Those are pretty clear words. Preaching is a great challenge and the Bible is filled with a wealth of material for good preaching. Shame on those who take each other's words and claim they received them from God. Early in my ministry I attended a Monday morning pastor's conference. All the pastors were describing what they had preached about the day before. One of the men said, "When better sermon books are published, I'll preach better sermons." He got the laughs he was after. I did not think it was funny then, and I still do not. When all a preacher has to preach are his own words, and all the inspiration he has is his own dreams, he had better not preach! False prophets hear their own voice. True prophets hear the voice of God.

Jeremiah went to the root of the trouble. The false prophets had not been in the counsel of the Lord. They had not been there because God had not called them. If they had been there, they would have heard God's message and would be proclaiming it.

Their dependence on their dreams brought about a lack of dependence on God. Unfortunately, the prophet who had the most brilliant dream would be the one the people would follow the most. Jeremiah saw all around him a faulty spiritual revelation of God. To Jeremiah, the dream was to the word of the Lord, as chaff is to the wheat.

There was a note of both realism and sarcasm in Jeremiah's words, "The prophet that hath a dream, let him tell a dream; and he that hath my word, let him speak my word faithfully" (Jer. 23:28). Jeremiah wanted the people to compare what a dreamer said with what the true prophet said. He would be aware that within his soul was God's word committed to him as the bearer of the message.

Because the false prophets were not in the counsel of the Lord, their preaching had no direct relationship with God. Jeremiah meant that his God was the true God of the covenant, not a little local god whose presence, purpose, and power was limited. God was, and is, not a next door sort of deity, or a god with whom one can become chummy. He is instead the majestic, sovereign God of all the universe, whose presence pervades everything. He is eminent and transcendent. There is a woe on those who presume to go when God has not sent them and when, in fact, he has not called them. Those prophets claim to preach God's words when really they are a pack of lies. They cannot escape their encounter with God. This passage suggests the question, "How big is your God?"

Jeremiah took note of all of this impious familiarity with the Word of God. It bred in Jeremiah a profound contempt and scorn. There was and is a presumptuousness about those who suppose they always understand God clearly and act as if God is their little private possession. There is an arrogance with which some people judge other's doctrine. God said, "Am I a God at hand, saith the Lord, and not a God afar off?" (Jer. 23:23). God keeps his divine distance and the more people presume upon his nearness the farther away he becomes. At the same time, God's infinite nearness is such that a man cannot hide his true motives. God is both holy and near.

The latter part of the twentieth century has brought an increasing overfamiliarity with God. To an extent, this has always been true, but it seems to be increasing. I recall an elderly gentleman in my home church, when I was growing up, who the pastor would call on to lead in prayer. When he prayed, I remember it sounded to me as if he knew the very thoughts of God and he was giving God a little help with all of his busy work. Once in awhile I find myself in the company of some fellow ministers who have no problem plunging right into the middle of other people's conversation. They talk glibly and easily about God's will. They punctuate their sentences with "praise God" and "praise the Lord." I have watched some religious music personalities on television sometimes caress the microphone lovingly, as if it were some kind of representative of God. All of this has always been extremely difficult for me. I have always found it rather difficult to pray and extremely difficult to presume upon God in prayer. I believe strongly in prayer. I practice it daily. I could not live without the fellowship with God provided by prayer. Yet I do not talk to God like I would talk to my roommate.

Preaching for me is the same experience. It is different from a lecture. The true prophet has been in the awesome presence of God. The message he then brings is not some other person's ideas or his own dreams, it is God's message.

That was what Jeremiah was saying. Jeremiah's preaching was that of a true prophet. The word on his heart and in his mouth was a word of fire. He had tried to call back his people, but they would not listen. His preaching then became God's message of judgment. The fire of judgment contained in Jeremiah's word to Judah was the fire of God's displeasure with his people. That was different from the false prophets who went about saying that all was well. It is easy to see who was the most popular. It is also easy, in retrospect, to see who was the true prophet. Jeremiah said there is a difference. There is a difference between dreams and reality. It is the difference between straw and wheat. Jeremiah charged the false prophets with being immoral, not knowing God, and having no message for the people. These are three accusations which today's man of God must take seriously. False prophets were careless of their responsibilities. Rather than raise the moral standards of the people they lowered them because they participated in sin. They did not have much knowledge of God. Because they did not understand his nature, they thought he loved Israel in a particular way and would bless them no matter what the people did. Jeremiah knew God in an intimate way, understood his nature, and knew that he must break away from the people who had spurned him, even if it meant the loss of those who preferred the message of the false prophet.

There is a clear illustration here of the false prophets clinging to tradition and dogma. Their messages were meaningless. Human lives were not changed and blessed as a result of them. On the other hand, Jeremiah, the true prophet, fearlessly, recklessly, and most of all, boldly, sought to proclaim the Word of God.

God's true word can be compared to a burning fire. Jeremiah

knew this in his own soul and it was like a hammer shattering a rock. It is dynamic. The false prophet, because he has no word from God, is tempted to steal the words of the authentic prophet, to preach someone else's sermon, say someone else's word. When a prophet speaks what he claims to be a revelation from God, but knows in his soul that no such revelation has been received, he is a fraud and God is opposed to him. This is a searching, penetrating, and unanswerable, prophetic analysis. No matter how pious or ministerial a preacher sounds, if his sermons are stolen, or did not come from God, they are not a revelation from God. Jeremiah censored the false prophets. He judged them responsible for the superficial optimism and the insensitivity to social and ethical issues. They were responsible for the moral and spiritual corruption of his countrymen. They were false prophets.

God tests the heart and it was because the false prophets did not have God's Word in their hearts that they were counterfeit preachers. What they did have in their hearts were lies. They prophesied the deceits of their own hearts and spoke about their own dreams. God had not sent them or even spoken to them. They were false prophets because as they told their dreams they caused the people to go after other gods.

That brings back the question I started with: When the messages sound genuine, how can you tell if someone is a real prophet of God? No one has a right to set a judgment upon someone else's call to preach the gospel. Many people have supplied their lists to help people recognize the true prophets of God. The following is mine.

1. The true prophet is one called by God. It is old and overworn, but remains true, that people do not choose to serve God, God chooses people. They serve him in response to his initial call to them. Those who are genuinely called will have an insight into the character of God and God's claims upon his people. The false prophet will have no such claim. In a time when some men are casting about for a career in the "helping professions" with some of them opting for the ministry, it is a good time to reaffirm again that no one ought to undertake the awesome responsibility of a preacher of God's Word unless one is called. Jeremiah could not have survived all that he did had he not felt this terrific sense of God's call.

2. The person, who is a true preacher, will be sensitive to human needs. This is the kind of person who does not manipulate or use people for his own purposes. Manipulation is the pattern of the world. The minister who falls into that trap is headed for a fall. Jeremiah did not use his people, he hurt for his people, cried over his people, yet, he spoke the truth to his people. Jeremiah was less involved in politics and more involved in preaching. Good lessons for God's prophets today.

3. The true prophet or preacher is aware that life is a sermon just as well as the messages he preaches. There is a demand for a high moral standard on the part of God's servant. In many ways the moral standard is no different from that of any other Christian, but there is a sense of leadership, stewardship, and example which the true preacher of God's Word sets.

4. The true prophet tries to effectively communicate the Word of God. He is not dogmatic, but open. He is willing to search for new truth and examine all revelations in the light of that particular truth. He respects the views of others, while insisting that others respect his views. False prophets usually see only one side and they are convinced that they are right and all others are wrong. There are false prophets on the scene today.

5. The true prophet is motivated by love and led by the Holy Spirit. He does not desire position or possessions. He does not have the urge to preach so that someone will hear him. His motivation is love for people and his desire to let the Spirit of God lead him.

6. The man of God, or the prophet of God, has a deep knowledge of God's full revelation in Jesus Christ. He knows that the gospel is the remedy for sin. He has a deep conviction that trust in Christ will bring peace to the conscience, purity to the mind, strength to the will, hope to the heart, and loving acceptance in the presence of God. The true prophet knows what God has done for him and knows what God can do for others. This is the reason he cannot keep silent. The fire that burns in his bones requires him to preach the message.

7. The true prophet has a deep knowledge of Christ. This is not just an acquaintance with the character of Jesus, nor a belief in truths about him, but a personal, experiential knowledge of Christ. The authentic true prophet knows that Christ died for him, redeemed him, accepted him, and gave him eternal life. He is in love with Christ so much that love constrains him to tell others. This is why he cannot keep silent. Loving Christ leads to loving all people, for Christ loves all people as much as he loves any one person.

A deep knowledge of the sin of his people and a knowledge that God wanted to forgive and redeem that sin consumed Jeremiah and all other great prophets like him. Jeremiah was a man of many moods. He rose and fell like the sun coming up and going down on any day. Often he was depressed and discouraged. But whenever the chips were down, Jeremiah came down on the side of God, loving his people and wanting them to be redeemed from their sins.

It is possible to recognize true prophets because they are God's gift to his people. Where the true prophet of God proclaims God's Word there is harmony and fellowship. True, prophetic, bold preaching brings about right relationships between God and people. True prophets boldly proclaim God's message in troubled times.

9
The Word of the True Prophet
Jeremiah 28:1-17

Everyone today is familiar with the sight of demonstrators. In the comfort of their living rooms Americans have watched, by means of television, massive demonstrations regarding one issue or another. In relative comfort and total uninvolvement many people watched parades as other people sought to act out their frustration and demonstrate their desire to see a certain action cease or take place. Most people have also seen demonstrations personally. It may have been an isolated person walking around the convention hall to protest a certain speaker, workers on strike for higher wages or better fringe benefits. Everyone is familiar with the sight of people symbolically acting out their message.

The prophet of the Lord, Jeremiah, on a number of occasions acted out the Word of God. He did it no more graphically than the incident in the passage of Scripture on which this sermon is based. To understand the incident in chapter twenty-eight it is necessary to know what led to it. That is recorded in the previous chapter.

Jeremiah had attempted to assess the political situation of his day through a sermon that was made up of both word and symbol. Nebuchadnezzar had placed Zedekiah on the throne of Judah. Zedekiah was too weak a leader for such turbulent times. He was surrounded by inexperienced advisors. Some favored staying close to Babylon. There were others who wanted to revolt and cast their lot with Egypt. Many people in Judea did not recognize Zedekiah as king; they still regarded the exiled Jehoiachin as the legitimate king. There were also a number of prophets who preached rebellion and others who predicted an end to the Babylonian rule.

There seems to have been a political meeting in Jerusalem and various small countries discussed revolt against Babylon. Nothing came of the meeting. Jeremiah opposed it. Zedekiah played both sides of the fence. He sent representatives to the meeting, but he also went to Babylon to pledge his loyalty to Nebuchadnezzar. It was against this backdrop that Jeremiah presented his message.

Jeremiah showed up at one of the meetings wearing a plough-man's ox-yoke around his neck. The yoke which Jeremiah was instructed to make and use in his symbolic action (Jer. 27:2) was like those used on an ox. It was made of a wooden yoke bar with leather thongs which came down under the neck. Apparently only one yoke was used.

The prophet declared that the yoke was a symbol of submission to Nebuchadnezzar of Babylon. He stated in his sermon that God was still in control of world events and that God was working out his pur-pose in history. However, he claimed that it was God's will at this time that the people submit to the yoke of Babylonian domination. He said the period of yielding to Babylon would last until Babylon's time of reckoning arrived. He urged his people not to fight against his message for to do so was to fight against God.

There were other prophets in the land besides Jeremiah and many of them were preaching that God's people should rebel and fight. Some were saying that the time was right to rebel. They were appeal-ing to the spirit of nationalism and rebellion to rise against Nebuchad-nezzar and his forces. These prophets were reminding people that they were God's peculiar people and that if they rose up in rebellion God would be with them. "Wrong," said Jeremiah, "To survive you must submit to Babylon.

The other prophets opposed Jeremiah's preaching. They assured the people that Babylonia's power would be broken. They claimed that soon both the exiles and the Temple furnishings would return. One prophet, Hananiah, had a time-table. He said:

"Thus speaketh the Lord of hosts, the God of Israel, saying, I have broken the yoke of the king of Babylon. Within two full years will I bring again into this place all the vessels of the Lord's house, that Nebuchadnezzar king of Babylon took away from this place, and carried them to Babylon: And I will bring again to this place Jeconiah the son of Jehoiakim king of Judah, with all the captives of Judah, that went into Babylon, saith the Lord: for I will break the yoke of the king of Babylon" (Jer. 28:2-4).

That was what the people wanted to hear. Public opinion was with Hananiah and his fellow prophets. Jeremiah was on the other side.

Jeremiah was a one man protest movement. It is not hard to imagine the stir that he must have created in Jerusalem. It was probably difficult for him, because it was very much out of character for this sensitive man of God. Yet he was concerned for his people and concerned enough to communicate to them God's message. No one could ever accuse Jeremiah of not communicating. His commitment to fulfilling his call was firm and his message was obvious. Jeremiah preached a sermon to Zedekiah, the king, and preached the same message to his priests and people. He urged them to stop listening to those who were urging rebellion and appealing to their nationalism. He said they should pray that their country would yield to the will of God so that everything else they believed holy would not be carried into a foreign land by Nebuchadnezzar. Jeremiah was coming more and more into conflict with the popular prophets of his day. Hananiah claimed that God had spoken to him also and he had a different message. Hananiah said, "Thus speaketh the Lord of hosts, the God of Israel, saying, I have broken the yoke of the king of Babylon" (Jer. 28:2). Hananiah probably was a leader among the prophets. When Jeremiah confronted Hananiah, Jeremiah was wearing the yoke. It was in the presence of the priest and others that Hananiah said he had received a revelation from God. He said that in a short time, two years, God was going to break the yoke of Babylon, bring back home the captives, return the Temple furnishings, and restore the rightful king, Jehoiachin, to the throne.

This presented a real dilemma to the people. They were hearing two prophets, both claiming to know and be sensitive to God's word, proclaiming God's message. How does someone handle different messages that claim to be from God? During the time I was preparing these sermons a young man came by my study to tell me of his radical transformation experience. He told me that, among other things, God had revealed a message to him. God had also revealed the place where that message was to be delivered, and it was my pulpit. There are not many things in life which I am jealous of, but my pulpit is one. I take seriously the sacred responsibility of proclaiming God's Word. Whenever I am not the one doing the preaching I want to be sure that the messenger in the pulpit is a faithful preacher of the gospel of Jesus Christ. Further questioning of this young man convinced me that he had a number of problems and I suggested that when God impressed me with the same message, namely that he was to be the preacher, I would consent and allow him to preach. In the meantime I could not allow him the use of the pulpit for his own propaganda. He put up no argument and left. I later learned he tried the same thing in a number of churches.

The people hearing Hananiah and Jeremiah concluded that one of them certainly had misinterpreted what God was saying to them. Jeremiah listened to Hananiah's words and replied to them "Amen: the Lord do so: the Lord perform thy words which thou has prophesied, to bring again the vessels of the Lord's house, and all that is carried away captive, from Babylon into this place" (Jer. 28:6). Jeremiah listened and said perhaps it was true. Jeremiah had no answer for Hananiah at the moment. In fact, he seemed to be saying that with all his heart he hoped the things Hananiah had predicted were true and that they would come about. This was a good picture of Jeremiah's character. It showed a man of no clerical self-righteousness, with no desire on his part to immediately jump to the defensive and prove himself right and Hananiah wrong. He did not challenge Hananiah to a debate. In fact, he said, "Amen, I hope your message is right." Then he walked away.

Jeremiah wanted to be sure that he had God's word before he spoke. He knew that God was not controlled by a prophet, but that the prophets were to be led by God.

God cannot be pulled out of a person's pocket like a dollar for personal use. Jeremiah knew he did not have a corner on all of God's truth. For the time being he wanted to be sure that he spoke God's truth. So he left. As much as he had walked with God, and as close as he had tried to live to God, still he wanted to be sure that he had God's word. For the moment, God was not saying anything to Jeremiah. So Jeremiah didn't speak; he walked away.

In some ways the last days of the Lord Jesus were like that. There must have been a feeling of awesome, almost unbearable, silence at Calvary. There God's Son was crucified and God did not seem to be saying anything. There was no army of angels who came to rescue him from the cross. Even when the scoffers cried, "If you are the Son of God come down from the cross," there was silence. God kept his silence that day. It was a difficult time. The disciples did not understand. Those who had accepted his challenge to follow him did not understand. No one seemed to know what God's word was that day, so they said nothing. In fact, many of them ran away.

Jeremiah did remind Hananiah that prophets stood in the stream of tradition in which true prophets spoke about judgment. Therefore, the burden of proof lay on Hananiah. This should not be interpreted to mean the entire message of all of the prophets before Jeremiah had been one of doom. There were hopeful messages as well as messages of judgment. Jeremiah was simply saying that the usual message of the prophets included threats of punishment. Jeremiah was saying that in prophesying doom he was more in the line of early prophets than those, like Hananiah, who prophesied welfare, prosperity, and happiness. He was saying that history would have to vindicate the prophet like Hananiah and his message, or else he would prove to be a false prophet.

True prophecy is always ethical in content and it relates to the contemporary situation in which people live. Jeremiah's people were

living in a state of rebellion against God and it appeared to him that
the prophetic word from God called for an up-front denunciation of
their sins, and a proclamation of the judgment to come unless they
repented. Jeremiah had difficulty with Hananiah's lighthearted fore-
cast of an easy victory and a changed circumstance without any call
for a moral transformation.

However, Jeremiah had a problem. He had a problem that a lot of
preachers have. His problem was that Hananiah's message sounded
more religious than his own. Hananiah's message sounded like what
the people wanted to hear. He was using the right words and the
people were responding. Jeremiah did not sound much like a
preacher.

I surrendered to the call to the ministry when I was eighteen years
old. Looking back on that event, it is obvious that I knew little about
the various functions of the ministry. To be truthful, I had a rather
glorified image of the pastor which was shattered pretty quickly. One
of the things I promised when I began preparation for the ministry, I
have tried to keep through the years. I never could understand how a
person could talk one way in ordinary conversation and then sound
entirely different when he went into the pulpit to preach. So, I said I
would never be guilty of using what I called "preacher language." I
have always tried not to change my voice when I go into the pulpit. I
do not believe there is any such thing as holy language, although
there are a lot of people who think a message becomes peculiarly
God's because of the way the spokesman pronounces certain words.
I categorically reject that.

That was Jeremiah's problem. Hananiah sounded a lot more religious than Jeremiah. He probably sounded more official, too. He
spoke in the house of the Lord and in the presence of the priests. He
was somewhat an official spokesman and what's more, he said what
the people wanted to hear. Hananiah represented the God everybody is looking for, the God who just happens to like all of the things
everybody happens to like. Whenever I read about Hananiah I think

about the man who told me that I ought to go hear a successful preacher. He said about him, "He's a Bible preacher and you ought to listen to him." I did, one time. Just saying "God bless you" a whole lot and talking about "the Word of the Lord" without ever proclaiming it, does not make a person a Bible preacher. The God of the Bible does not have to accommodate himself to any preacher's message. Preaching or prayer becomes a farce when all a person wants is for God to get him out of trouble and bless the things he wants.

People do like to listen to prophets who say what they want to hear. The people were like that in Jesus' day that was one of the reasons why he taught that before people pray for what they want, they should pray, "Thy will be done" (Matt. 6:10). Jesus had a problem because he did not say everything the people wanted to hear. That was why the religious groups of his day were upset with him. He upset their hopes, their pious organizations, and their preachers. They wanted a messiah who would liberate them from the Roman yoke of occupation and Jesus was just not that person. They were upset because he did not organize an army or start a war. Those who did cluster about Jesus and became his followers were really upset when he let himself be crucified. Jesus refused to let pious words be a substitute for a meaningful life. That is one of the reasons they crucified him. All of Jesus' life said, "Time will tell who is right."

That is still wise advice. Some churches today spend more time trying to keep members from joining other established churches and complaining about other's orthodoxy, rather than proclaiming their own message. Occasionally some of the preachers even get on radio and television and say things that are not true. Some of my colleagues become extremely upset. They want to answer these false prophets and challenge them. This does little good. I have always found the counsel of "time will tell" to be good advice.

One of the questions that honest people must always wrestle with is: how do you know you are right? That was Jeremiah's problem. For the moment he did not say anything. Jeremiah believed that the

Word of God would be self-authenticating. He was content to do nothing until God spoke. That is good advice for both the pew and the pulpit.

Jeremiah's reaction must have infuriated Hananiah because he broke the yoke from the neck of Jeremiah and said, "Thus said the Lord; Even so will I break the yoke of Nebuchadnezzar king of Babylon from the neck of all of the nations within the space of two full years" (Jer. 28:11). Hananiah broke the yoke which Jeremiah had used to symbolize subjection to Babylon for a long period. In effect he was saying that his message of prophecy canceled out Jeremiah's. What was Jeremiah's reaction? "And the prophet Jeremiah went his way" (Jer. 28:11). Jeremiah probably went his way because he wished Hananiah's message could be true. He wanted to be saved for himself and for his people also. He could not accept Hananiah's message, and yet it was not the moment to challenge it. So he waited.

Jeremiah waited until he heard from the Lord. When he heard, he replied with boldness, "Then the word of the Lord came unto Jeremiah the prophet, after that Hananiah the prophet had broken the yoke from off the neck of the prophet Jeremiah, saying, Go and tell Hananiah, saying, Thus saith the Lord; Thou hast broken the yokes of wood; but thou shalt make for them yokes of iron" (Jer. 28:12-13).

Jeremiah had an answer both for his nation and for Hananiah. For Hananiah, he said, "Hear now, Hananiah; The Lord hath not sent thee; but thou makest this people to trust in a lie" (Jer. 28:15). The message for the nation was: Instead of the yoke of wood that could be broken, God was going to give them an iron yoke that would not break. Those who had refused to submit, but had counseled revolution as implied in Hananiah's prophecy, would have to live in total subjection to Nebuchadnezzar.

There is a sense in which all of God's people have yokes. They are the yokes of responsibility for oneselves, others, and God. If people refuse to live under those yokes, it is part of the plan of God that the people themselves make the yokes harder and heavier. This is part of what Jesus meant when he said, "For my yoke is easy, and my burden is light" (Matt. 11:30). Its wearer is yoked to the power of God. Jeremiah also reminded his people that the terrible yoke of iron would have to be worn in the place where God would allow his people to be taken, Babylon. It would be Babylon that would be their home, the place where they would find their meaning and their future.

Hananiah was a false prophet. He had perverted the word of the Lord and made the people trust in a lie. The personal message of Jeremiah's prophecy to Hananiah was that he would die because he had uttered rebellion against the Lord. After silently waiting on the word of God, Jeremiah realized Hananiah's motives. Hananiah was responding to the prestige of his office, and speaking the hopes and dreams that his people wanted to hear. When Jeremiah brought Hananiah's motives out into the open, the false prophet could not stand the true light of God's truth.

Two prophets were engaged in open disagreement, both claimed to speak the word of the Lord, both tried to speak with earnestness and sincerity, both used the same "Thus says the Lord," both engaged in a symbolic act (the wearing of the yoke and the breaking of it), yet both could not be right. Jeremiah was the true prophet. Hananiah was a false prophet. There is that question again. How do you know? How can the people know? The answer is still the same as Jeremiah's. Time vindicates the true prophet. How do we identify the genuine voices today? There are a lot of Hananiah's and only a few Jeremiah's around. It is the Jeremiah's who are proclaiming the bold message. That message can take many faces, but it usually comes out in a form that the people do not want to hear.

It may be a message that calls for renewed, bold commitment to loyalty to the church of Jesus Christ. This is a time when people belong to many organizations and give their allegiance to many causes, many of them good. Some preachers are saying as long as the purposes are good, ethical, and moral, God approves. They say,

"Spread yourself around." The true prophet is still calling God's people to a deeper involvement in the greatest organization in the world, the church.

The true preacher is calling for a bold approach to Bible study. Not a casual opening of a quarterly a few minutes before a Sunday School class on a Sunday morning, not a misguided Bible study group that spends more time looking at footnotes than at the actual text, but a genuine Bible study that attempts not to worship the words, but the God who reveals himself through those words. There are some who claim that there are many revelations from God and people should become conversant with all of them and study some of them along with the Bible. The true prophet still proclaims that God's Word comes first.

The true prophet is still the one teaching that the tithe belongs to God and that the local church is the storehouse to which it should be brought. It is easy to become a popular preacher by approving of the rationalizations that any good project supported with their funds is part of their tithe. The truth is that the tithe belongs to God and his people have given no offering until that tithe is brought to him. It takes bold courage and bold believing to practice this truth, but those who do practice it find the windows of heaven opened up for them and a great blessing poured on them (Mal. 3:10).

The bold preacher is the one calling God's people to a deeper level of prayer. Prayer is conversation with the Creator of the universe, prayer involves speaking and listening, prayer is intelligible and understood both by the one praying and by the one hearing the prayer. There is a great deal of truth to be said for living in a posture of prayer and having one's whole life bathed in prayer. It is still true, however, that there must be specific times of prayer, and that requires discipline and sacrifice. It takes a bold message to declare that.

There is one thing of which Christians can be sure. There will always be a voice that says what some people want to hear and people are certainly free to follow that voice. There will always be the Jeremiah-type voices which are much harder to follow. Christians must seek honestly to do whichever is God's way.

There comes to my mind again that scene at Calvary. God was saving the world and no one noticed. No one heard the message because there were so many voices. God is still saving the world today and still speaking through his bold prophets. We need to hear them. They are speaking God's message in troubled times.

10
Does God Forget?

Jeremiah 31:31-34

Jeremiah was a great preacher. He was a bold preacher of God's message in troubled times. Of all his preaching, he said nothing that was more significant than the words recorded in Jeremiah 31:31-34.

Some scholars think that this is the most important single teaching of Jeremiah. Many consider it the climax of his prophetic preaching. It is certainly a mountain peak in the Old Testament. This bold Old Testament message has had a profound effect on the New Testament. A number of commentators have referred to this passage as an example of a "gospel before the gospel."

This noble prophecy of Jeremiah came in the midst of a time of destruction. The words must have been spoken during, or shortly after, the tragedy of 587 when all of Jeremiah's predictions had come true. Everything he loved or cherished was either in chaos or gone, except his relationship with God. It was that relationship that sustained him.

As Jeremiah reflected on the destruction of his land and the scattering of his people, he concluded that the situation was desperate because the people had broken the covenant. The old covenant had been broken. It was not God's fault that it was broken, it was the fault of the people. "Which my covenant they brake, although I was a husband unto them, saith the Lord" (Jer. 31:32). In the midst of this kind of desperate situation what could help? Only a bold act and that is exactly what God did. In one of the boldest acts imaginable he gave his people a new covenant.

This new covenant would not be written on stone tablets, as the old, but on the fleshly tablets of human hearts. It is interesting to contrast the old covenant with its negative prohibitions and the new covenant of which Jeremiah spoke. The verbs in the old covenant (Ex. 20) say "thou shalt" and "thou shalt not." In Jeremiah the beautiful words of God are "I will make ... I will put ... and write," and "I will forgive."

This new covenant of which Jeremiah spoke would succeed because its success was guaranteed by God. The old covenant had revealed Israel's inability to meet God's requirements. The people of Israel thought they could keep it, but century after century they demonstrated that they could not. Later, in times of captivity and return, they would want to reaffirm the old covenant, but Jeremiah saw beyond the old covenant to the new day and the call for a new covenant. God was determined to restore Israel (Jer. 31:27-38). Jeremiah made it clear that in any dealings with Israel God would work through the individuals so that each person would be held responsible only for his own sins (31:29-30). Under the new arrangement a person would not be able to blame his fate on anyone except himself. This was how the Lord had always dealt with people, but the people of the old covenant had confused their national solidarity with personal responsibility for their sins. Jeremiah saw it and distinguished the difference.

As a pastor, I feel a burden for the people God has allowed me to serve. There are times when I worry about some of the members of our church. There are occasions when I hurt and sometimes cry for their human plight. Each day I lift them up to God in prayer. When they succeed in some area of life I rejoice. When they fail I feel a sense of burden and some of their guilt. Finally, however, I must conclude that they are responsible for their own acts. Any pastor who constantly carries the burden of his congregation with him everywhere he goes will eventually crack up. I cannot take the failure of every person home with me at night or my own life would soon turn to failure. God does not want me to do that. My responsibility, under

God as a pastor, is to proclaim the bold message of God to the best of my ability and point men and women in the direction God would have them to go. I am to lead them, as a shepherd leads the sheep, to make the right decisions; but, in the final analysis, the decision is theirs and they must bear the responsibility.

When I first began preaching I had great problems with revival meetings. I felt personally responsible for the success of the revival meeting. When people did not respond to the invitation, when lives were not being saved and changed, I found it difficult to sleep at night. I prayed long and agonizing prayers asking God to bring about revival. Then one day it dawned upon me that my stewardship in preaching was to proclaim to the best of my ability God's Word. My preaching, for good or bad, did not determine the response. The response was determined by the Holy Spirit. I should preach and then leave the results in God's hands. Once I settled this I found a lot more joy in preaching revivals.

It is true that all people suffer, to some degree, because of the sins of their fathers. But it is also true that no one is held responsible for any sins but their own.

Christians should not overlook the fact that they are still part of the whole family of human beings. Jeremiah wanted to remind his people that like the old covenant the new covenant was to be made with the house of Israel, the whole house of Israel. The new covenant would transcend their sense of national identity but there would be a sense of group solidarity that would remain. The individual was the focal point of the new covenant's religious experience but it was not the individual apart from the community. The Old Testament never distinguishes the individual from the group. Rugged individualism in religion is not biblical.

Occasionally I hear someone claim that they are an "independent" Christian. I am never sure I understand exactly what they mean, but if they mean they are Christians doing their own thing without any need for participation in the life of the community, then they are mistaken. There are no "Lone Rangers" in Christianity. Christians are all part of one another. In the Christian experience there really is no such person as an independent. Christians are all interdependent upon one another. Christians are part of one another and desperately need each other.

There is an eschatalogical dimension to the words of Jeremiah regarding the new covenant. It marked the end of one way God dealt with his people and it inaugurated a new method. "Behold, the days come, saith the Lord, that I will make a new covenant" (Jer. 3:31). This obviously refers to a new type of relationship. The new part of the new covenant is what God does. God will put his will directly into the heart of a person so that all of the external methods of communication will no longer be necessary. Jeremiah did not mean that there would no longer be the necessity for teaching or preaching. He was talking about the work of the Holy Spirit in a person's heart. The day was coming when God would both illuminate people and give them the ability to respond.

The impulse to keep the covenant will come from within. "After those days, saith the Lord, I will put my law in their inward parts, and write it in their hearts; and will be their God, and they shall be my people" (Jer. 31:33). Jeremiah also stressed that it will be an individual matter. "And they shall teach no more every man his neighbour, and every man his brother, saying, Know the Lord: for they shall all know me, from the least of them to the greatest of them, saith the Lord" (Jer. 31:34).

The new covenant is one of grace. It comes from the heart of God. The impulse to keep it comes from within, so that people can serve God because they want to, not because they felt they have to or ought to. The new covenant will be an individual matter.

Jeremiah emphasized that this new covenant was to be permanent. The old covenant was broken again and again but this one will last. It will last because God himself guarantees the outcome of it. This is the good New Testament teaching that once a man places his hand in the hand of Jesus Christ he is a child of God forever. The person who knows Jesus Christ as personal Lord and Savior has a relationship with God that will endure. Once a man gives his heart and life to God he is never lost, he is found. If he could be lost again the new covenant would fail, and it does not.

Then there occurs one of the most beautiful statements in the Bible. Through the prophet Jeremiah, God says "For I will forgive their iniquity, and I will remember their sin no more" (Jer. 31:34b). God was saying "I will forget their sins." That is startling and amazing.

Like many of you, I sometimes am a forgetful person. I do not usually forget things of major importance, and do try to keep my appointments on time. My wife says that I get so involved with things at the church that I forget little things I am supposed to bring home from the store, or messages I am supposed to deliver. I plead guilty. Everyone forgets things at times.

Many people have great difficulty remembering names. It is extremely embarrassing to forget names. Sometimes it is understandable because the passing of years and experiences tend to blur names and faces together. But there are some people who have difficulty remembering names that they should have learned only a month ago. That is embarrassing.

Sometimes people forget promises. One of the reasons today's society is in such sad shape is because people do not keep promises. When a young couple stands before me to be married and I listen to them repeat their marriage vows, I cannot help but wonder if they mean to keep their promises. The number of divorces today indicates that many people are not serious about marriage promises. Many people have made promises to God that they have forgotten. Nearly every pastor can recount experiences like this one. Early in my present pastorate, I encountered a distraught husband in a local hospital. His wife was undergoing major surgery. She had become suddenly and violently ill. The surgeons feared for her life. Filled with guilt and frightened that his wife would die, this young husband began telling me about all of the things he had done wrong, especially in his relationship to God and his church. At the end he blurted out, "If God will save her and give her back to me, I promise that I will be faithful to the church and give God his tithe. God can count on me." His wife did survive the surgery and I was naively pleased because I thought we had another fine couple in our church. I was mistaken. That kind of foxhole promise does not last.

Human beings forget all kinds of little things. They forget to say thank you. They forget to say I love you a lot. They forget that sometimes a gentle touch of one human being to another speaks volumes. They forget.

Everyone forgets. That's just human. But God? How can God forget? God forgets, he is not forgetful. God never forgets his world. The world operates on a twenty-four hour basis and every day arrives on time and the night pulls in on schedule. God does not forget his world. He remembers lilies and sparrows. God does not forget prayers either. Christians tend to pray for something for a short period and then when the answer does not come, they sometimes forget about the prayer. Have you ever been riding down the street in an automobile, when suddenly you realized that something you had been praying for, but had not mentioned in your prayers lately, had been answered sometime ago? God is not forgetful. But he forgets. That is what Jeremiah said.

What does God forget? Ironically, the Bible pictures God as forgetting the thing people want most forgotten, sins. God forgets sins not because he is getting older, nor because he has many things to do, but because he wants to. People carry around an enormous amount of guilt. Guilt is brought about by a number of things. Many people have problems coping with life because as children they did not measure up to their parents' expectations, and even as adults they find it difficult to be pleasing to their parents. This is an unrealistic and unhealthy attitude toward life and is often used as a cop-out, but it does contribute to a sense of guilt.

Many people are legalists. They read the Ten Commandments and because they do not measure up to some of them, they conclude that they are guilty. They read other parts of the Bible that tell about Jesus saying people should love their enemies, but they do not. They know they should love one another or themselves and they do not. Their guilt continues to pile up. People are overloaded with personal guilt and add to it every day.

The message of God's redeeming love, however, is that God is able both to forgive and forget sins. When is God able to forgive? When people let him. Here is the new element of this new covenant. It was perfectly fulfilled in the life and ministry of Jesus Christ, who gave up his life to make the words of Jeremiah become reality. Now, thousands of years removed from Jeremiah, the truth of his words is affirmed because of the action of Jesus Christ.

The moment a person says yes to the claims of Jesus Christ on their life, they become a Christian. The moment they recognize they are a sinner and cannot save themselves, and they turn in trusting faith and obedience to claim the promises of God, he creates a new covenant. God does not shut his eyes and pretend that the situation does not exist. He takes people just like they are and he forgets their sins because they have trusted his grace and his Son, Jesus Christ, who is the sin bearer.

To the struggling human who asks the question, how can a sinner possibly have fellowship with God, the answer comes back, because God forgives. There is no life-changing fellowship apart from the forgiveness of sins. The human predicament is serious and only God can do something about it. That is what the cross does. It actualizes in history the saving act of God. Jeremiah's message preached God's grace. The life of Jesus Christ demonstrates God's grace. Christ's offer to follow him, in faith, in a new covenant relationship is one of grace. The same grace which brought Israel into being also created the new Israel through faith in Jesus Christ.

Jeremiah knew that the religion based on the old covenant had failed. He recognized that his people failed to grasp the reality of their individual responsibility under the old covenant. There was no hope of renewing the old covenant. A new one had to take its place. The new covenant would be personal and inward. It would be manifested universally and spiritually. God would be seen clearly and would make his will known to those who turned to him in faith. The new covenant would be a covenant that brought moral cleansing and a sense of divine fellowship.

Israel had to be transformed from the inside and it was this future action of God that Jeremiah proclaimed. God would forgive the people of all their past sin. The years of disobedience would be wiped out. God would receive his people back in a new fellowship containing new commandments. They would not be like the commandments given at Sinai. It would be an inner law, written upon their hearts. The new commandment would be the inner motivation of all conduct, so that every person could be obedient and love God.

This was the vision of the future that Jeremiah saw as the finest of Judah's people marched off to captivity. There is always a future with God even when it looks to mankind like the end. There is a resurrection that brings victory out of the seeming defeat of the cross. The hope for the future is with God and his actions. That was what Jeremiah preached and lived.

Jeremiah did not live to see his prophecy fulfilled. What he did experience was the truth that God never left him. When he began his ministry God told Jeremiah, "Be not afraid of their faces: for I am with thee to deliver thee" (Jer. 1:8). When Jeremiah's faith faltered God would remind him of his promise. It was the presence of God that sustained him to the day of his death. Jeremiah found God to be faithful in every way.

The most beautiful fulfillment of this covenant can be found in the words recorded in the Gospel of Luke.

"And when the hour was come, he sat down, and the twelve apostles with him. And he said unto them, With desire I have desired to eat this passover with you before I suffer: For I say unto you, I will not any more eat thereof, until it be fulfilled in the kingdom of God. And he took the cup, and gave thanks, and said, Take this, and divide it among yourselves: For I say unto you, I will not drink of the fruit of the vine, until the kingdom of God shall come. And he took bread, and gave thanks, and brake it, and gave unto them, saying,

This is my body which is given for you: this do in remembrance of me. Likewise also the cup after supper, saying, This cup is the new testament in my blood, which is shed for you" (Luke 22:14-20).

The expression "new testament" literally means new covenant. Jesus said to his disciples gathered in the upper room that the new covenant predicted by Jeremiah was now being instituted in him. There was no better way to describe the work of the Lord than through this new covenant.

Paul contrasted the old covenant and the new covenant in 1 Corinthians 3. The sermon recorded by the author of Hebrews is an application of the words of Jeremiah.

> For if that first covenant had been faultless, then should no place have been sought for the second. For finding fault with them, he saith, Behold, the days come, saith the Lord, when I will make a new covenant with the house of Israel and with the house of Judah: Not according to the covenant that I made with their fathers in the day when I took them by the hand to lead them out of the land of Egypt; because they continued not in my covenant, and I regarded them not, saith the Lord. For this is the covenant that I will make with the house of Israel after those days, saith the Lord; I will put my laws into their mind, and write them in their hearts: and I will be to them a God; and they shall be to me a people: And they shall not teach every man his neighbour, and every man his brother, saying, Know the Lord: for all shall know me, from the least to the greatest. For I will be merciful to their unrighteousness, and their sins and their iniquities will I remember no more. In that he saith, A new covenant, he hath made the first old. Now that which decayeth and waxeth old is ready to vanish away (Heb. 8:7-13).

The writer of Hebrews was saying that the new covenant was better in every way than the old. It not only set up a goal, it gave the believers the power to realize it in their life. He would go on to say that the new covenant had an eternal high priest, instead of a human priest, and that it was based on a perfect sacrifice, instead of animal sacrifices. The new covenant was made up of realities, not a mere shadow of things, and a perfect victory would come because of the sacrificial death of the Lamb of God, Jesus Christ, the new covenant.

Jeremiah never saw the new covenant become a reality. He was in the group that the writer of Hebrews wrote about, "Yet they did not receive what God had promised, because God had decided on an even better plan for us. His purpose was that only in company with us would they be made perfect" (Heb. 11:39-40, TEV).

I like the idea of being in the company of Jeremiah. No one ever brought God's message in troubled times better than this courageous prophet.

I live and work near a major medical center, the Bowman-Gray School of Medicine and North Carolina Baptist Hospital. I served for several years on the board of trustees of that fine healing institution. As a pastor, I often visit patients there who have had heart surgery. Many of them have literally been given extensions of life by the skill of heart surgeons. Their hearts will last longer but they are not new. Only God can give a new heart and that is what he does in and through the new covenant.

"This shall be the covenant.... I will put my law in their inward parts, and write it on their hearts; ... I will forgive their iniquity, and I will remember their sin no more" (Jer. 31:33-34).

Isn't that beautiful? "I will remember their sin no more." That is God's message in troubled times.

11
Sermon Outlines

Repentance, True and False
Jeremiah 3:21 to 4:4

   I. The People Long for Something Better (3:21)
- A. The people are confused.
- B. They know they have perverted their way.
- C. They have followed false gods and forgotten the true God.

  II. God's Call in Response to Their Cry (3:22)
- A. If the people will turn to God in genuine repentance, he will heal them.
- B. Backsliding children eventually experience shame and disappointment.

 III. The People Speak Again (3:22b-25)
- A. They acknowledge they have followed a delusion.
  1. Is this genuine repentance?
  2. Is this merely regret?
- B. This likely is a picture of shallow repentance.
  1. It is more remorse than repentance.

 IV. God Calls for Real Repentance (4:1-4)
- A. The emphasis is on "return unto me" (v. 1).
  1. Repentance means to come all the way back to God.
- B. True repentance requires repudiation of idolatry and recognition of God's Lordship.